Roll Me Over

Edited by Harry Babad

Compiled and Collected at The University of Illinois
by the Illini Folk Arts Society

Oak Publications, New York

Music Sales Limited, London

*To "Papa" Bill Godsey, without whose hospitality there would have been
a lot less picking and singing; and to John Walsh, Jim Hockenhull, Paul Sampson
and Victor Lucas, among the many prime movers, not unmoved.*

Cover illustration by Aristide Maillol

Book design by Jean Hammons

This book Copyright © 1972 by Oak Archives,
An Imprint of The Music Sales Group

ISBN: 978-0-8256-0067-8

Exclusive Distributors:
Music Sales Corporation
257 Park Avenue South, New York, NY 10010 USA
Music Sales Limited
14-15 Berners Street, London W1T 3LJ England
Music Sales Pty. Limited
120 Rothschild Street, Rosebery, Sydney, NSW 2018, Australia

Printed in the United States of America by
Vicks Lithograph and Printing Corporation

TABLE OF CONTENTS

(Cont'd)

A Prefatory Note

This is a singer's collection, as opposed to a collection for the folklorist. In most cases, we have combined two or more versions to get the most complete text and singable tune we could. Still, a few notes are in order, partly to lend an air of spurious respectability to the book, and partly because one of the collectors is a pedant and likes to annotate songs. Beyond these notes it is hard to comment on sources, because almost no research has been done on these songs.

First, about the scope of the book; this is primarily a collection of dirty songs. It is customary at this point to make some pious reference to the *Ulysses* and *Lady Chatterly's Lover* court decisions. No such defense will appear here. The songs are not great literature, and if they can be defended, it must be on other grounds. Most of the songs here are funny. It is hard to find a ribald song that is not humorous. It is well-known that humor—real laughter—and suggestiveness do not cohabit. The dirty song aims to get a belly laugh, not a lecherous snicker. The last thing a pornographer wants his audience to do is laugh; the last thing the singer of bawdy songs wants is to make his audience . . . well, restless.

In spite of the nature of their work, the editors claim title to at least a modicum of morality, and beg the reader to remember that he already knows several of these songs, and has sung them with alcoholic gusto on more than one occasion. The reader is not depraved; neither are we. But we, like the reader, know that occasionally we need to purge ourselves of our less acceptable emotions in a below-stairs songfest with "the boys." Sometimes nothing else will, as Tom D'Urfey put it, "purge the melancholy."

Some of these songs are straight wish fulfillment. Some are incredibly nasty, and disgust even the relatively shockproof editors, who include them as horrible examples, with reluctant admiration for the nerve of the first man to sing them publicly; with them goes the dismal thought that these bathroom-wall ditties also have a crumb, however far decayed, of the truth. But there is also a goodly number of sprightly, good-humored, tuneful, and (we believe) funny songs, some of them fit for the most maidenly ear.

Some of the songs, among them some of the best, never mention sex. They are concerned instead with drink, about which the singing folk have fewer really pessimistic thoughts. As the Irish song has it, "Whiskey, you're the divil, ye're leading me astray . . . ah, whiskey, ye're me darlin', drunk or sober." A few non-lecherous, non-drunken songs are included because their stoutly masculine spirit, fine melody, and poetically respectable text make them fitting companions for their more ribald brethren.

If the songs in this book are any indication, human beings are a pretty disillusioned group, but able to stand up to their problems with a kind of dignity best exemplified, perhaps, in this stanza from an Irish drinking song in which the singer sees death coming for him.

> I fear that old tyrant approaching,
> That cruel and remorseless old foe,
> But I lift up me glass in his honor;
> Take a drink with old Rosin the Beau.

ELIZABETHAN SONGS

During the time of Elizabeth, England was freeing itself from the rigid bonds of feudalism. The Renaissance was reaching its full flower of maturity; with it came an intense curiosity about man and the universe. Sex was no longer something to abhor, but something natural in the life of man. This resulted in the healthy lack of self-repression and the candor which is evident in these songs. They are not songs to snicker at behind the cowshed; Shakespeare, Marlowe and Johnson had many passages in their plays which were just as libidinous as anything printed here.

These songs are no less ribald than the songs of other periods; however, they are less coarse. The Scots take a great delight in the story and its humorous setting; the Americans enjoy coarse words and startling impossibilities, but with the Elizabethans the joy is clearly in the telling. The stories are simple, uncomplicated by many double reverses and twists of the plot. Instead, emphasis is placed on extended metaphors, puns, and double entendre.

"The Lusty Young Smith" (7, 8, 18) is an example of an extended pun in which the work and tools of the blacksmith trade are used to describe a seduction in complete detail. In "A Wanton Trick" (7, 8, 18), musical instruments rather than blacksmith's tools are used for the same end. In "Character of A Mistress" (7, 8, 18), the singer metaphorically describes his love at great length only to discover that he can describe her more fully in only two words. The melody of this last song has come down to us as "The Ballade of Miss Bailey" or "The Hunters of Kentucky."

Other songs, such as "Of Chloe and Celia" (7, 8, 18), have none of these traits. They are not humorous, but are more nearly laments—laments that our human shortcomings keep us from enjoying sex perfectly.

All but three of the songs in this section originated from *The Pills to Purge Melancholy*, edited by Thomas D'Urfey and published in 1719. "The Butcher and the Tailor's Wife" (24) is from the singing of Paul Clayton, while the tune is an extra melody to "The Handsome Cabin Boy" which was lying around, and was added here when one of us took a personal dislike to the colorless melody which Clayton sang. Both "Character of a Mistress" and "The Fornicator" (9, 10, 18) were obtained from the singing of Ed McCurdy, and all the songs except "The Butcher and the Tailor's Wife" and "Blow the Candles Out" (7, 17-1, 18, 19, 24) may be heard on the "Dalliance" series of records on the Elektra label, sung most excellently by McCurdy. Some of the songs from the "Dalliance" series have recently appeared in a collection entitled *Song Book of Wit and Mirth*, published by Hargail Music Press in 1963. This unusual version of "Blow the Candles Out" can be heard on a Stinson recording of "The Pills to Purge the Melancholy" sung by Will Holt. This recording also contains a number of other songs taken from the D'Urfey collection.

* These numbers refer to the books and records listed in the bibliography and discography at the back of this book. Numbers *1-16* are books or song collections and numbers *17-26* are records.

CHARACTER OF A MISTRESS

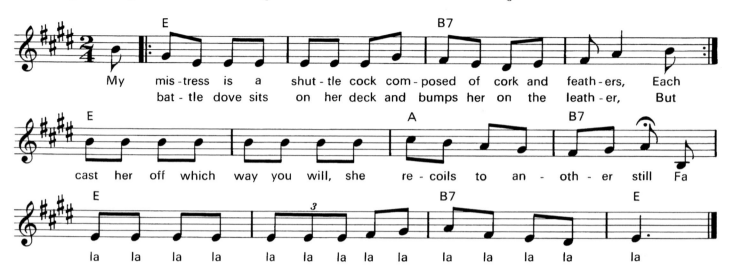

My mis-tress is a shut-tle cock com-posed of cork and feath-ers, Each
bat-tle dove sits on her deck and bumps her on the leath-er, But

cast her off which way you will, she re - coils to an - oth - er still Fa

la la la la la la la la la la la la la

My mistress is a shuttle cock
Composed of cork and feathers,
Each Battledove sits on her deck
And bumps her on the leather.
But cast her off which way you will,
She recoils to another still,
    Fa la la la la la la la
    Fa la la la la la la la.

My mistress is a tennis ball
Composed of cotton fine,
She's often struck against the wall
And banded underline.
But if you would her wish fulfill
You'd pop her in the hazard still.

My mistress is a virgin hole
And little cost will string her,
She's often reared against the wall
For everyone to finger.
But if you would your mistress please,
You'd run division on her keys.

My mistress is a cunny fine
And of the finest skin.
And if you care to open her
The best part lies within.
Yet in her cunny burrow may
Two tumblers and a ferret play.

My mistress is a tinder box
Would I had such a one.
Her steel endureth many a knock
Both by the flint and stone.
And if you stir the tinder much
The match will fire at the touch.

But why should I my mistress call
A shuttlecock or bauble,
A virgin hole or tennis ball
Which things are variable.
But to commend I'll say no more,
My mistress is an arrant whore.

A WANTON TRICK

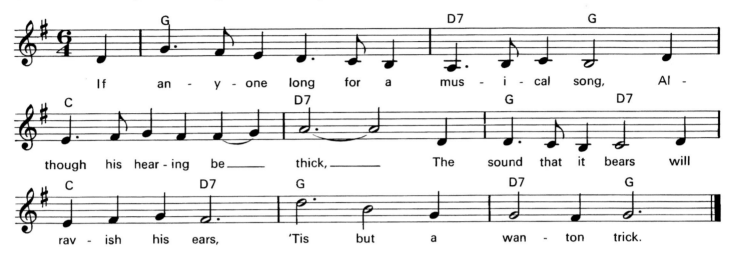

If anyone long for a musical song
Although his hearing be thick,
The sound that it bears will ravish his ears—
'Tis but a wanton trick.

A pleasant young maid on an instrument played
That knew neither note nor prick.
She had a good will to live by her skill—
'Tis but a wanton trick.

A youth in that art, well seen in his part,
They called him Darbyshire Dick,
Came to her a suitor and would be her tutor—
'Tis but a wanton trick.

He pleased her so well that backward she fell
And swooned as though she were sick,
So sweet was his note that up went her coat—
'Tis but a wanton trick.

The string of his viol she put to the trial,
'Till she had the full length of the stick.
Her white-bellied lute she set to his flute—
'Tis but a wanton trick.

Thus she with her lute and he with his flute
Held every crochet and prick.
She learned at her leisure yet paid for her pleasure—
'Tis but a wanton trick.

His viol string burst, her tutor she cursed;
However, she played with the stick.
From October to June she was quite out of tune—
'Tis but a wanton trick.

And then she repented that e'er she consented
To have either note or trick;
For learning so well made her belly to swell—
'Tis but a wanton trick.

All maids that make trial of a lute or a viol,
Take heed how you handle the stick;
If you like not this order, come try my recorder—
'Tis but a wanton trick.

THE FORNICATOR

You jov - ial boys, __ who know the __ joys, __ the bliss - ful joys __ of lov - ers, __ And dare show it __ with daunt - less __ brow_ What-e'er the lass __ dis - cov - ers. __ I pray draw near_ and you shall hear, and wel - come in a fra - ter, __ I've late - ly been__ un - quar - an - tined__ a true born for - ni - ca - tor. __

You jovial boys who know the joys,
The blissful joys of lovers.
And dare show it with dauntless brow
Whatever the lass discovers,
I pray draw near and you shall hear,
And welcome in a frater-
I've lately been unquarantined,
A proven fornicator.

Before the congregation wide
I passed the muster fairly.
My handsome Betsy by my side,
We gat our ditty rarely.
My downcast eye by chance did spy
What made my mouth to water,
Those limbs so clean where I between
Became a fornicator.

With woeful face and sigh of grace
I paid the buttock higher.
That night was dark and through the park
I could not but convey her.
A parting kiss—what could I less?
My vows began to scatter.
Sweet Betsy fell—fol lol der rol—
I am a fornicator.

But by the fun and moon I swear,
And I'll fulfill, I'll carol it,
That while I own a single crown
She's welcome to a share o't.
My roguish boy, his mother's joy
And darling of his pater—
I for his sake the name will take,
A hardened fornicator.

INTENSE EXCITEMENT!

A Lusty Young Smith

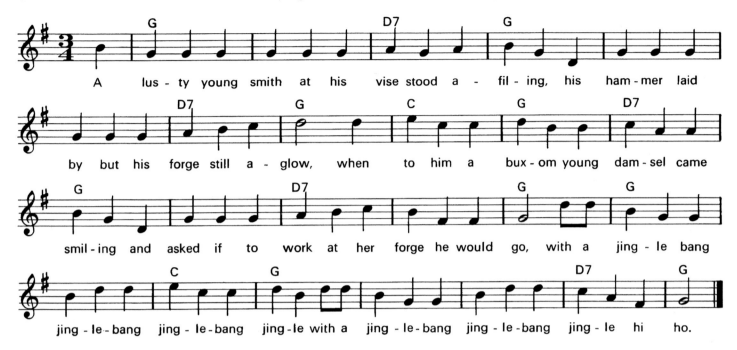

A lus-ty young smith at his vise stood a-fil-ing, his ham-mer laid
by but his forge still a-glow, when to him a bux-om young dam-sel came
smil-ing and asked if to work at her forge he would go, with a jing-le bang
jing-le-bang jing-le-bang jing-le with a jing-le-bang jing-le-bang jing-le hi ho.

A lusty young smith at his vise stood a-filing,
His hammer laid by but his forge still aglow,
When to him a buxom young damsel came smiling
And asked if to work at her forge he would go.
    With a jingle, bang jingle, bang jingle, bang jingle,
    With a jingle, bang jingle, bang jingle, hi ho!

"I will," said the smith, and they went off together
Along to the young damsel's forge they did go,
They stripped to go to it, 'twas hot work and hot
    weather;
She kindled a fire and she soon made him blow.

Her husband, she said, no good work could afford her;
His strength and his tools were worn out long ago.
The smith said, "Well mine are in very good order,
And now I am ready my skill for to show."

Red hot grew his iron, as both did desire
And he was too wise not to strike while 'twas so.
Quoth she, "What I get, I get out of the fire,
Then prithee, strike hard and redouble the blow."

Six times did his iron, by vigorous heating,
Grow soft in the forge in a minute or so,
And often was hardened, still beating and beating,
But each time it softened it hardened more slow.

The smith then would go; quoth the dame, full of
    sorrow,
"Oh, what would I give, could my husband do so!
Good lad, with your hammer come hither tomorrow
But, pray, can't you use it once more, ere you go?"

THE JOLLY MILLER

The old wife she sent to the miller her daughter to grind her grist quick-ly and
mil-ler so worked it that in eight months af-ter her

so re-turn back, the bel-ly was filled___ as well as her sack the

mil-ler so pleased her that when she came home she gaped like a
hoy-dened, she scamp-ered she hol-lowed and

stuck pig and stared like a mome, she whooped, and all the day long, this,

this was her song, "Was ev-er a maid-en so le-ri-com-pooped?

The old wife she sent to the miller her daughter
To grind her grist quickly and so return back;
The miller so worked it that in eight months after
Her belly was filled as well as her sack.
The miller so pleased her that when she came home,
She gaped like a stuck pig and stared like a mome,
She hoydened, she scampered, she hollowed and
    whooped,
And all the day long, this, this was her song,
"Was ever a maiden so lericompooped?"

"Oh Nellie," cry'd Celie, "thy clothes are so mealy,
Both backside and belly are rumpled all o'er,
You mope now and slabber, why what the pox ails
    you?
I'll go to the miller and know you the more";
She went and the miller did grinding supply,
She came cutting capers a foot and half high,
She waddled, she straddled, and hollowed and
    whooped,
And all the day long, this, this was her song,
"Was ever a maiden so lericompooped?"

Then Mary, mild Mary, the third of the number
Would fain know the cause they so jigged it about;
The miller her wishes long would not encumber
But in the old manner the secret found out.
Thus Celie and Nellie and Mary the mild
Were all about harvest time heavy with child,
They danced in the hay and they hollowed and
    whooped,
And all the day long, this, this was their song,
"Were ever three maidens so lericompooped?"

And when they were big they did stare at each other
And crying, "Now, sisters, what shall we do?"
For all our young bantlings they have but one father
And they in month time all will come to town too.
Oh, why did we run in such haste to the mill
To Robin, who always the toll dish would fill?
He bumped up our bellies, then hollowed and
    whooped,"
And all the day long, this, this was their song,
"Were ever three maidens so lericompooped?"

12

WOULD YOU HAVE A YOUNG VIRGIN?

Would you have a young virgin of fifteen years, you must
tickle her fancy with sweets and dears ever toying and
playing and sweetly, sweetly sing a love sonnet and charm her fears.
Wittily, prettily talk her down chase her and praise her if
fair or brown, sooth her and smooth her and tease her and
please her and touch but her smicket and all's your own.

Would you have a young virgin of fifteen years,
You must tickle her fancy with sweets and dears,
Ever toying and playing and sweetly, sweetly,
Sing a love sonnet and charm her fears.
Wittily, prettily, talk her down,
Chase her and praise her if fair or brown,
Soothe her and smooth her and tease her and please
    her
And touch but her smicket and all's your own.

Do you fancy a widow well known in a man,
With a front of assurance come boldly on,
Let her rest not an hour but briskly, briskly,
Put her in mind how time steals on.
Rattle and prattle although she groan,
Rouse her and touse her from morn till noon,
Show her some hour you're able to grapple,
Then get but her writing's and all's your own.

Do you fancy a lass of a humour free
That's kept by a fumbler of quality.
You must rail at her keeper and tell her, tell her,
Pleasure's best charm is variety.
Swear her more fairer than all the town
Try her and ply her when cully's gone,
Dog her and jog her and meet her and treat her
And kiss with two guineas and all's your own.

BLOW THE CANDLES OUT

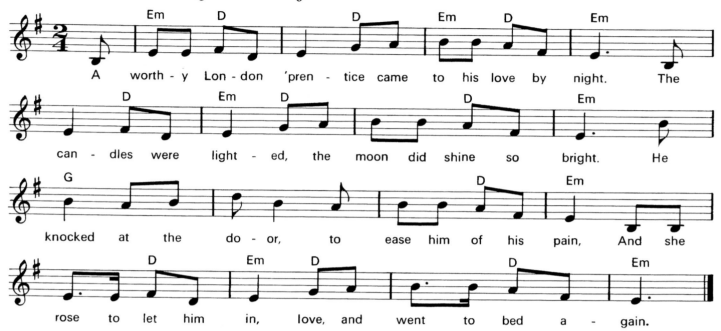

A worth-y Lon-don 'pren-tice came to his love by night. The can-dles were light-ed, the moon did shine so bright. He knocked at the do-or, to ease him of his pain, And she rose to let him in, love, and went to bed a-gain.

A worthy London 'prentice came to his love by night.
The candles were lighted, the moon did shine so bright.
He knocked at the door to ease him of his pain,
And she rose to let him in love, and went to bed again.

He went into the chamber where his true love did lie.
She quickly gave consent for to have his compani',
She quickly gave consent the neighbors to keep out,
"So take away your hand love and blow the candles out."

"I would not for a crown love, my mistress should it know.
I'll in my smock step down and I'll out the candle blow,
The streets they are so nigh and the people walk about,
Some may peep in and spy, love, let's blow the candles out.'

"My master and my mistress upon the bed do lie,
Enjoying one another, so why not you and I?
My master kissed my mistress without a fear or doubt,
And we'll kiss one another, but let's blow the candles out."

"I prith-thee speak most softly, about what thee hast to do
It's sad that either parting should make our pleasure new.
For kissing one another we'll make no evil route,
So let us now be silent and blow the candles out."

What yet he must be doing, he could no longer stay.
She strove to blow the candle out and pushed his hand away.
The young man was so hasty to lay his arms about.
Still she cried "I pray love let's blow the candles out."

As this young couple sported, the maiden she did glow.
How the candle went out alas I do not know.
Did she act in a flash, my mistress and my dame?
But what this couple did, alas I dare not name.

The Jolly Tinker

A come-ly dame of Is-ling-ton had got a leak-y cop-per, The hole that let the liq-uor run was want-ing of a stop-per, A jol-ly tin-ker un-der-took and prom-ised her most fair-ly with a thump thump thump and a Knick, Knack, Knock, to do her bus-iness rare-ly.

A comely dame of Islington had got a leaky copper;
The hole that let the liquor run was wanting of a stopper.
A jolly tinker undertook and promised her most fairly
(With a thump, thump, thump and a knick, knack, knock)
To do her business rarely.

He turned the vessel to the gound, said he, "A good old copper,
But it well may leak for I have found a hole in it that's a whopper.
But never doubt a tinker's stroke, although he's black and surly,
(With a thump, thump, thump and a knick, knack, knock)
He'll do your business rarely."

This man of mettle open wide his budget's mouth to please her,
Says he, "This tool I've oft employed about such jobs as these are."
With that the jolly tinker took a stroke or two most kindly,
(With a thump, thump, thump and a knick, knack, knock)
He did her business finely.

As soon as he had done the feat he cried, " 'Tis very hot-o
This thrifty labour makes me sweat; give me a cooling pot-o."
Says she, "Bestow the other stroke before you take your farewell,
(With a thump, thump, thump and a knick, knack, knock)
And you may drink a barrel."

Two Maidens Went A-Milking

Two maidens went a-milking one day,
Two maidens went milking one day,
And the wind it did blow high,
And the wind it did blow low,
And it tossed their pails to and fro,
It tossed their pails to and fro.

They met with a man they did know,
They met with a man they did know,
And they said, "If you've the will,"
And they said, "If you've the skill"
You might catch us a small bird or two,
You might catch us a small bird or two.

"Here's a health to the blackbird in the bush,
Here's a health to the merry, merry doe.
If you'll come along with me
Under yonder spreading tree
I will catch you a small bird or two." (2)

So they went and they sat 'neath a tree, (2)
And the birds flew round about;
Pretty birds flew in and out,
And he caught them by one and by two. (2)

My boys, let us drink down the sun,
My boys, let us drink down the moon,
Take your lady to the wood
If you really think you should—
You may catch her a small bird or two,
You may catch her a small bird or two.

OLD FUMBLER

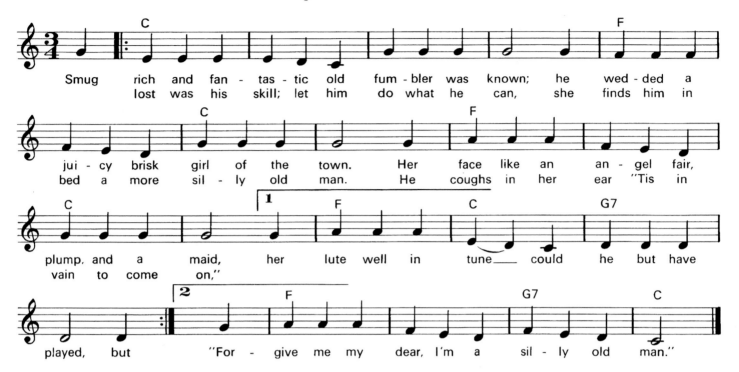

Smug rich and fan - tas - tic old fum - bler was known; he wed - ded a
lost was his skill; let him do what he can, she finds him in

jui - cy brisk girl of the town. Her face like an an - gel fair,
bed a more sil - ly old man. He coughs in her ear "Tis in

1
plump, and a maid, her lute well in tune___ could he but have
vain to come on,"

2
played, but "For - give me my dear, I'm a sil - ly old man."

Smug, rich and fantastic, Old Fumbler was known
He wedded a juicy, brisk girl of the town.
Her face like an angel, fair plump and a maid;
Her lute well in tune could he but have played.
But lost was his skill; let him do what he can,
She finds him in bed a mere silly old man.
He coughs in her ear, "'Tis in vain to come on,
Forgive me my dear, I'm a silly old man."

She laid his dry hand on her snowy white breast
And from those fair hills gave a glimpse of the best.
But, ah, what is youth when our life's but a span:
She found him an infant instead of a man.
"Ah, pardon," he cried, "That I'm weary so soon.
You have let down my bass, I'm no longer in tune.
Lay down that dear instrument, prithee lie still.
I can play but one lesson and that I play ill."

THE BUTCHER AND THE TAILOR'S WIFE

There was a poor old tail-or and in Lon-don he did dwell. He had a hand-some wife, and her name was Mar-y Bell. She went off to the mark-et, a bit of meat to buy, "What is your will dear Ma-dam" the but-cher did re - ply.

There was a poor old tailor and in London he
   did dwell,
He had a handsome wife and her name was Mary
   Bell,
She went off to the market, a bit of meat to buy,
"What is your will, dear madam," the butcher
   did reply.

"That joint of meat is what I wish, but I know it
   is too dear,
If you can find some scraps for soup it'll have to
   do I fear."
"I'll give to you that joint of meat, you need not
   think to buy,
But you must agree this night with me you'll lie."

The joint of meat was quick cut down, refuse it
   she did not,
Straighway she fetched it home and put it in the
   pot;
And when the tailor he came home she told him
   what she had,
The tailor leaped for joy and then his heart was
   very glad.

"But husband, oh, husband, I'll tell you how it
   must be,
This very night the butcher he has to lie with me;
So take your broadsword in your hand and hide
   beneath the bed
And the first man that enters, stab him till he's
   dead."

"I've never handled sword or gun, my dear and
   loving wife,
And butchers they are bloody dogs, I'm afraid
   he'll have my life."
"Oh, don't you be faint-hearted, have courage
   stout and bold,
And you'll have an honest wife and we'll keep the
   butcher's gold."

Now the butcher thinking it was time to see the
   tailor's wife,
And fearing they should form a plot or trick to
   take his life,
He got a brace of pistols loaded up the power and
   ball,
"The first man that molests me now, by heaven,
   I'll make him fall."

When the butcher he made in, she took him by
　　the hand,
She led him to the bed and said, "Now sir, I'm at
　　your command,"
He pulled out the pistols and laid them on the
　　bed,
The poor old tailor squeaked with fear and lay as
　　if quite dead.

But the butcher taking off his clothes to make his
　　joys complete,
He brushed against the broadsword's point and
　　ripped his trouser seat;
"Is this your husband under here, by God, I'll end
　　his life."
"O, spare me, sir," the tailor cried, "And you
　　may have my wife."

"You've done me harm," the butcher cried, your
　　life on one condition,"
"Oh, name it sir," the tailor begged, "Don't send
　　me to perdition."
The butcher took his trousers off and then to
　　save his life,
The tailor sewed his trousers while the butcher
　　had his wife.

OF CHLOE AND CELIA

Nothing than Chloe e'er I knew
By nature more befriended;
Celia's less beautiful, 'tis true,
But by more hearts attended.
No nymph alive with so much art,
Receives her shepherd's firing,
Nor does such cordial drops impart
To love when just expiring.

Why thus, ye gods, who cause our smart,
Do you love's gifts dissever?
Or why those happy talents part
Which could be join'd forever?
For once perform an act of grace,
Implor'd with such devotion;
And give my Celia Chloe's face,
Or Chloe, Celia's motion.

THE BAFFLED KNIGHT

There was a Knight and he was young, a-going a-long the way sir, _____ and there he met a la-dy fair a-mong the cocks ___ of hay sir; Down Der-ry Down. ___

There was a knight and he was young
A-going along the way, sir,
And there he met a lady fair
Among the cocks of hay, sir, down, derry down

Quoth he, "Shall you and I, lady
Among the grass lay down, o,
And I will take a special care
Of rumplin' of your gown, O"

"If you go along with me
Unto my father's hall, sir,
You shall enjoy my maidenhead
And my estate and all, sir."

He mounted her on a milk-white steed,
Himself upon another
And then they rid upon the road
Like sister and like brother.

And when she came to her father's house
All moated round about, sir,
She stepped straight within the gate
And shut this young knight out, sir.

"Here is a purse of gold," she said,
Take it for your pains, sir
And I will send my father's man
To go home with you again, sir.

And if you meet a lady fair
As you go through the town, sir,
You must not fear the dewy grass
Or the rumplin' of her gown, sir,

"And if you meet a lady gay,
As you go by the hill, sir,
If you will not when you may
You shall not when you will, sir."

THREE TRAVELERS

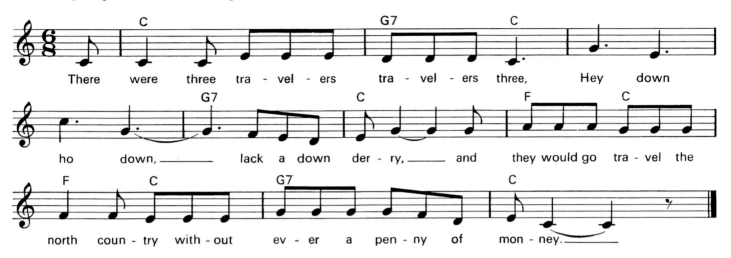

There | were | three | tra - vel - ers | tra - vel - ers | three, | Hey | down
ho | down, | lack | a | down | der - ry, | and | they would go | tra - vel | the
north | coun - try | with - out | ev - er | a | pen - ny | of | mon - ney.

There were three travelers, travelers three,
(Hey down, ho down, lack a down derry)
And they would go travel the north country
(Without ever a penny of money.)

At length, by good fortune, they came to an inn,
And they were as meery as e'er they had been.
Without ever a penny of money.

A jolly young widow did smiling appear
Who gave them a banquet of delicate cheer
Without ever a penny of money.

They drank to their hostess a merry full bowl,
She pledged them in love, like a generous soul,
Without ever a penny of money.

The hostess, her maid and cousin, all three,
They kissed and made merry, as merry could be,
Without ever a penny of money.

When they had been merry good part of the day
They called their hostess to know what to pay
Without ever a penny of money.

The handsomest man of the three, up he got.
He laid her on her back and he paid her the shot.
Without ever a penny of money.

The middlemost man to her cousin he went,
She being handsome, he gave her content
Without ever a penny of money.

The last man of all, he took up with the maid,
And thus the whole shot, it was lovingly paid,
Without ever a penny of money.

The hostess, the cousin and servant, we find,
Made curtsies and thanked them for being so kind,
Without ever a penny of money.

Then, taking their leaves, they went merrily out.
They're gone for to travel the nation about
Without ever a penny of money.

Of God,   Of Man,   Of the Divell.

SCOTS SONGS

"As in Italy, love is the great theme of Scots folk song, but unlike Italy, it is the act of love rather than the emotion which is celebrated."

—Ewan MacColl

The earthy vein of humor that runs through so much of Scots folksong has long been the bane of the serious and proper folklorists who collected them. Many were forced either to bowdlerize them beyond recognition or to include only the most colorless songs. However, a few collectors have managed to resist the middle-class temptation of the blue-nose pencil, and to them we owe the preservation of many of the most beautiful as well as the most humorous Scots songs.

It is to the efforts of Robert Burns, the great Socttish poet, that we owe most of the songs in this collection. Burns collected folksongs, and it was his wont to use some of these as a basis for his poems. "John Anderson, My Jo," "When Comin' Through the Rye," and others were originally based on folksongs. He collected the bawdiest of these in a manuscript (published posthumously), called *Merry Muses of Caledonia,* and we can be sure that he sang these songs over many a bonnie glass with his drinking cronies.

We're Gaily Yet

"Aillie" is a diminutive form for Elizabeth as well as being a word for ale. The tune is a popular Irish reel.

> We's a get gear — we'll all get wealth
> Meal pyock — bag for oatmeal (22)

Muirland Meg

The tune is also used for "The Laird O' Cockpen." (9, 10, 17-III, 20)

The Muckin' o' Geordie's Byre

This is probably the best known song in Eastern Scotland and no "boose-up" is complete without at least one rendering. The tune is a popular jig throughout Scotland and Ireland, where it is known as "Maggie Pickens."

Lea-rig auld croft — old small holding with grass fields
Grain was tint — pitchfork was lost   Siccan a sotter — such a mess
Roond the neuk — round the corner   Strae and neep — lay straw
Sweir — awkward   and pick turnips
Muckin' — removing dung   Greep — open drain in a byre
Besom was deen — broom was worn out   Neep — turnip
Posties sheltie — postman's pony   Midden dyke — wall around a dung heap
Byre — cowshed   Bumbees byke — bees nest (22)

The Carlton Weaver

The Calton woolen mills on the edge of Glasgow have been out of operation for many years, but this song continues to be sung. It is unusual (at least in this book) for the woman is used as a symbol, this time for whiskey, instead of the reverse. (14)

The Bonnie Wee Lassie Who Never Said No

MacColl in his liner notes says: "The scene is a drinking howff-part brothel, part pub. A man and a harlot make a night of it and he robs her. The choice of gin as a liquor suggests the early 1800's when every town in Britain had its Gin Lane. It is unusual for any other drink than whiskey to be celebrated in Scots song." Like several others in this section, the words are put to a popular jig tune. (22)

Beware of the Ripples, Young Man

This is full of sage advice. The ripples, it is said, are the king's evil, or scrofula. The melody is a variant of "The Campbells Are Coming." (20)

Eppie Morrie

Ewan MacColl said of the traditionally bloody Scots ballads that "The light ones are about attempted rape." By this standard, this classic ballad of the abduction and attempted marriage of Eppie Morrie must rank as one of the best of the "light ones." (14)

Tail Toddle

This song's charm lies in its absolute bluntness. "Plack" and "Boodle" refer to Scots coins.
(9, 10, 14, 20)

The Wind Blew the Bonnie Lassie's Plaidie Awa'

This was a great favorite in the bothies and is still sung. The melody is an old Irish song, "The White Cockade," said to be the last tune played in battle by the Irish pipes of war.

(22)

Who Will Mow Me Now?

The tune is "Comin' Through the Rye." To say that Burns' poem is merely a cleaning up of this song would be a grave injustice to his poetic genius. Nevertheless, the two songs are similar, both being about girls who have lost their laddie. "Who Will Mow Me Now" explains exactly why the lassie lost her laddie. (9, 10, 20)

The Cuckoo's Nest

This song is quite reminiscent of the Elizabethan songs and is at least old enough to qualify as one. (22, 17-IV)

John Anderson, My Jo

During the Reformation, there was a general and violent anti-Catholic sentiment in the British Isles, and nowhere was it stronger than in Scotland. Percy writes in his *Reliques*: "From the records of the General Assembly of Scotland called the *Book of the Universal Kirk*, p. 90, 7th July 1568, it appears that Thomas Bassendyne, printer in Edinburg, printed 'A Psalme buik, in the end whereof was found printit ane baudy sang, called "Welcome Fortunes" '."

It was common practice then to compose ridiculous and obscene anti-papist doggerel to the tunes of the favorite psalms of the Latin service. Much of this scurrilous poetry was set to beautiful melodies, and "John Anderson, My Jo" was originally one of those. Percy gives two verses of this song:

> *woman*
> John Anderson, my jo, cum in as ze gae bye
> And ze sall get a sheips heid weel baken in a pye;
> Weel baken in a pey, and the haggis in a pat;
> John Anderson, my jo, cum in, and ze's get that.
>
> *man*
> And hoe doe ze Cummer; and how hae ze threven;
> And how mony bairns hae ze? Wom. Cummer, I hae seven.
> Man. Are they to zour awin gude man? Wom. Na, Cummer, Na,
> For five of tham were gotten, quhan he was awa.

Percy explains that by the seven "bairns" were meant the seven sacraments, five of which were the "Spurious offspring of Mother Church." The first verse is a sarcastic reference to the rich living of the clergy. By the time the song reached Robert Burns, it had changed enough to give him the inspiration for his beautiful poem. We leave it for the reader to decide which version is the more poetic and beautiful. Meanwhile, this is the version which Burns collected. (9, 10, 20)

The Cooper of Dundee

Here is an example of an extended pun on the occupation of a cooper, or barrel-maker.

(9, 10, 20)

We're a' Jolly Fu'

This centuries-old song is the Scots equivalent of "Roll Your Leg Over" and, like that song, lends itself to ready improvisation. It is a great favorite at stag drinking sessions, where it's likely to go on indefinitely. Some vocabulary which might help:

Loose — louse	Puggie — frog
Moose — mouse	Cuddie — donkey
Deil — devil	Cheil — a man
Parritch pail — porridge pail	(22)

Green Grow the Rashes

In 1793, Robert Burns wrote to his publisher, "At any rate, my song, 'Green Grow the Rashes' will never suit. The song is current in Scotland under the old title, and to the bonnie old tune of that name." However, his song did suit, and became far better-known than the older song. This version is closer to the original. (*9, 10, 11, 17-IV, 22*)

The Keach in the Creel

MacColl got it from Grieg's *Traditional Ballads*. This bonnie ballad was long a favorite in the bothies, and has been collected in this country as well, almost unchanged (see *Abelard Song Book*). A "creel" is a large wicker basket. (*14*)

Nine Inch Will Please a Lady

Sing this sweetly, all you gentle lovers, for the melody is beautiful. (*9, 10, 20*)

Lassie Gathering Nuts

The equivocal last verse seems to require at least one more to explain it. Sorry, that's all there is. The tune is "Mormond Braes." (*10, 20*)

Duncan MacLeerie

This song is a relative of "Tom Bolynn" (p. 80). Ewan MacColl, a Scotsman, of course, says that they are both descended from a 16th century Scots song, "Tom O'Linn." (*10, 20*)

The Patriarch

This is to the tune of "Lassie Gathering Nuts." The Patriarch does his duty as he sees it, and who are we to say nay to the busy man? However, his concept of duty would make for an interesting discussion in any philosophy class. (*9, 10, 20*)

WE'RE GAILY YET

We're gai-ly yet, we're gai-ly yet, We're no ve-ry fu', but___ gai-ly yet, Then sit ye a while and tip-ple a bit, For we're no ve-ry fu', but we're gai-ly yet, Then up wi't your, up wi't your, ail-lie o. Up wi't your, up wi't your, ail-lie o, Then up wi't your, ail-lie, up wi't your, ail-lie, We'll a' get a roar in' fu'!

We're gaily yet, we're gaily yet,
We're no' very fu' but gaily yet,
Then sit ye a while and tipple a bit,
For we're no' very fu' but we're gaily yet.

    Then up wi't your, up wi't your Aillie-o.
    Up wi't your, up wi't your Aillie-o.
    Then up wi't your Aillie, up wi't your Aillie,
    We'll a' get roarin' fu'.

There were three lads and they were clad,
There were three lasses and them they had;
Three trees in the orchard are new sprung
And we's a' got gear enough, we're but young.

The one was kissed intil the barn,
Another was kissed upon the green,
The third had her back to the pease stack,
And the mow was up to her e'en.

Rin! Jock Thomson, ye maun rin,
Gin ye ever ran in your life;
There's a man wi' his hand in your meal-pyock
And another in bed wi' your wife.

Then awa Jock Thomson he did run
And he ran wi' muckle speed,
But before he'd run half o's length,
The loon had done the deed.

MUIRLAND MEG

Among our young lassies there's Muirland Meg,
She'll beg 'fore she'll work and she'll play 'fore
    she'll beg.
At thirteen her maidenhead flew on its way
And the door of her cage stands open today.
    And for a sheep's foot, she'll do it, she'll do it,
    And for a sheep's foot she'll do it, she'll do it,
    And for a ram's horn, she'll do it till morn,
    And merrily turn to and do it and do it.

Her rolling back eyes would thrill you through,
Her rosebud lips cry "Kiss me, come do,"
The curls and the links of her bonnie black hair
Would put you in mind there's more hiding elsewhere.

An armful of love is her bosom sae tender,
A span of delight is her middle sae slender,
A pretty white leg and a thumping white thigh,
And a fiddle near it to play by and by.

Love's her delight and kissing's her treasure,
She'll stick at nae price if you give her good measure,
As long as a sheep foot, large as a goose egg,
That is the measure of Muirland Meg.

THE MUCKIN' O' GEORDIE'S BYRE

In a leary old croft ayont the hill
Just roond the neuk frae Sprottie's mill
Trying a' his life the time to kill
Lived Geordie MacIntyre.
He had a wife as sweir's himself,
A dochter as black as old Nick in Hell—
There was plenty of fun awa' at the mill
At the muckin' o' Geordie's byre.
    Whaur the graip was tint, the besom was deen,
    The barra, it wouldna' row its leen,
    And siccan a sotter there never was seen
    As the muckin' o' Geordie's byre.

The dochter had to strae and neep
The auld wife started to swipe the greep,
When Geordir fell sklite on a rotten neep
At the muckin' o' Geordie's byre.
Ben the greep cam' Geordie's soo
And she stuid up ahint the soo;
The coo kickit oot, and o whit a stew
At the muckin' o' Geordie's byre.

The auld wife she was booin' doon
The soo was kickit on the croon
And shoved her heid i' the wifie's goon
And then ben thro' Geordie's byre.
The dochter cam' through the barn door,
And seein' her mither lat oot a roar,
To the midden she ran and fell ower the boar
At the muckin' o' Geordie's byre.

The bar he left the midden dyke
And oot he raced wi' Geordie's tyke
And then fell into the bumbee's byke
At the muckin' o' Geordie's byre.
The cocks and hens began to crow
When Biddy astride the soo they say,
The Postie's sheltie ran awa'
At the muckin' o' Geordie's byre.

28

A hunder years hae passed and mair,
Where Sprottie's was, the hill is bare;
The croft's awa', sae ye'll see nae mair
O' the muckin' o' Geordie's byre.
His fowk's a' deid and awa' lang syne,
Just whistle this tune tae keep ye in mind
O' the muckin' o' Geordie's byre.

THE CARLTON WEAVER

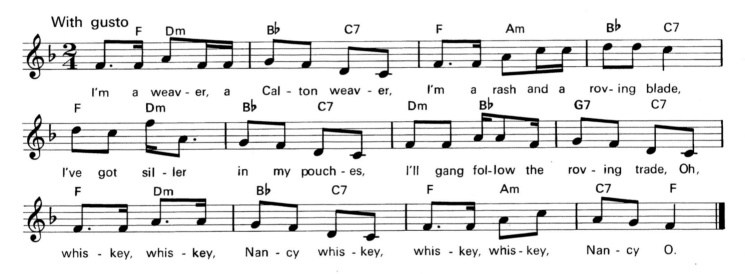

I'm a weaver, a Carlton weaver,
I'm a rash and a roving blade,
I've got siller in my pouches,
I'll gang follow the roving trade,
    Whiskey, whiskey, Nancy Whiskey,
    Whiskey, whiskey, Nancy-o.

As I cam' in by Glesca city,
Nancy Whiskey I chanced to smell,
So I gaed in, sat doon beside her,
Seven lang years I lo'ed her well.

The mair I kissed her the mair I lo'ed her,
The mair I kissed her the mair she smiled,
And I forgot my mither's teaching,
Nancy soon had me beguiled.

I woke up early in the morning,
To slake my drouth it was my need,
I tried to rise but wasna able,
Nancy had me by the heid.

"C'wa, landlady, whit's the lawin.
Tell me whit there is to pay."
"Fifteen shillings is the reckoning,
Pay me quickly and go away."

As I went oot by Glesca city,
Nancy Whiskey I chanced to smell;
I gaed in drank four and sixpence,
A't was left was a crooked scale.

I'll gang back to the Carlton weaving,
I'll surely make the shuttles fly,
I'll make more at the Carlton weaving,
Than ever I did in the roving way.

Come all ye weavers, Carlton weavers,
A' ye weavers where e'er ye be;
Beware of whiskey, Nancy Whiskey,
She'll ruin you as she ruined me.

THE BONNIE WEE LASSIE WHO NEVER SAID NO

I came to a cross and I met with a lass, says
I "My wee lass are ye wil-ling to go take your share of a gill?" She says,
"Yes, sir, I will, for I'm the wee las-sie who nev-er says "No."

I came to a cross and I met with a lass,
Says I, "My wee lass are ye willing to go
Take your share of a gill?" She says, "Yes, sir, I will,
For I'm the wee lassie who never said no."

For it's into an ale-hoose we merrily did go,
And we never did rise till the cock it did crow;
And it's glass after glass we merrily did toss,
Tae the bonnie wee lassie who never said no.

The landlady opened the door and came in
She opened the door and came in with a smile;
She lifted a chair and with freedom did say
"Here's a health to the lass who can jog it in style."

"So bring us some liquor, oh lassie!" she cried.
"To cheer up our spirits, I doubt they are low."
"Oh it's no' whit ye'll dae, bring a bottle or twae
Tae the bonnie wee lassie who never said no."

The drink they took in being the best o' the gin,
And being, myself, dead sober to be;
And it's glass after glass they merrily did toss
Till the lass and the landlady filled hersel' fu'.

"Look into my pocket," the lassie did say,
"There is two and sixpence to pay for my bed,
And for laying me down, you owe me a crown,
Look into my pocket," the lassie she said.

I put my hand in her pocket and five pound I took,
Says I to myself, "I will bundle and go."
So I bade her goodbye but she made no reply,
The bonnie wee lassie who never said no.

BEWARE OF THE RIPPLES, YOUNG MAN

Freely, not too fast

I ad - vise ye be - ware of the rip - ples young man; I ad -
vise ye be - ware of the rip - ples young man tho the sad - dle be soft, ye
need na ride oft, for fear that the thrust - ing be - quile you young man.

I advise ye beware of the ripples, young man,
I advise ye beware of the ripples, young man,
Tho' the saddle be soft, ye need not ride oft,
For fear that the thrusting beguile you, young man.

I advise ye beware of the ripples, young man, (2)
Though music be pleasure, take music in measure
Or you may lack wind in your whistle, young man.

I advise ye beware of the ripples, young man, (2)
Whate'er they demand, do less than you can,
The more will be thought of your kindness, young man.

I advise ye beware of the ripples, young man, (2)
If you would be strong, and wish to live long,
Dance less with your chest to the nipples, young man.

EPPIE MORRIE

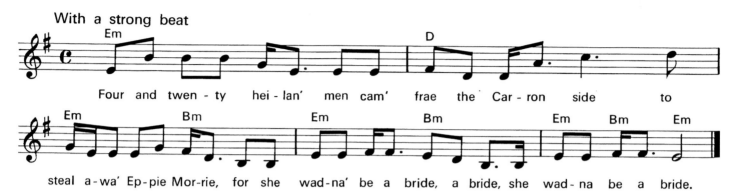

With a strong beat

Four and twen-ty hei-lan' men cam' frae the Car-ron side to steal a-wa' Ep-pie Mor-rie, for she wad-na' be a bride, a bride, she wad-na be a bride.

Four and twenty hielan' men
Cam' frae the Carron side,
To steal awa' Eppie Morrie
For she wadna' be a bride, a bride,
She wadna' be a bride.

Then oot it's cam' her mither,
It was a moonlicht nicht;
She couldna see her dochter
For the waters shone sae bricht, sae bricht,
The waters shone sae bricht.

Haud awa' frae me, mither
Haud awa' frae me!
There's no a man in a' Strathdon
Shall wedded be wi' me, wi' me,
Shall wedded be wi' me.

They've taken Eppie Morrie then
And a horse they've bound her on,
And they have rid to the minister's hoose
As fast as horse could gang, could gang,
As fast as horse could gang.

Then Willie's ta'en his pistol out
And put it to the minister's breast;
Oh, marry me, marry me, minister,
Or else I'll be your priest, your priest,
Or else I'll be your priest.

Haud awa' frae me, Willie!
Haud awa' frae me!
I daurna avow to marry you
Except she's as willing as thee, as thee,
Except she's as willing as thee.

They've taken Eppie Morrie then
Sin better couldna be,
And they hae rid ower Carron side
As fast as horse could flee, could flee,
As fast as horse could flee.

Then mass was sung and bells were rung
And they've gang awa' to bed,
And Willie and Eppie Morrie
In ane bed they were laid, were laid,
In ane bed they were laid.

He's ta'en the sark frae off his back
And kicked awa' his shoon,
And thrawn awa' the chaumer key
And naked he lay doon, lay doon,
And naked he lay doon.

Haud awa' frae me, Willie,
Haud awa' frae me!
Before I lose my maidenhead
I'll try my strength wi' thee, wi' thee,
I'll try my strength wi' thee.

He's kissed her on the lily breist
And held her shouthers twa,
And aye she grat and aye she spat
And turned to the wa', the wa',
And turned to the wa'.

A' through the nicht they wrassled there
Until the licht o' day,
And Willie grat and Willie spat
But couldna' stretch her spey, her spey,
He couldna' stretch her spey.

Then early in the morning
Before the licht o' day,
In came the maid o' Scallater
Gown and shirt alane, alane,
Gown and shirt alane.

Get up, get up, young woman
And drink the wine wi' me.
You micht ha' ca'd me maiden
For I'm sure as hale as thee, as thee,
For I'm sure as hale as thee.

Weary fa' you, Willie, then,
That ye couldna prove a man;
You micht hae ta'en her maidenhead,
She would hae hired your hand, your hand,
She would hae hired your hand.

Haud awa' frae me, lady,
Haud awa' frae me,
There's no' a man in a' Strathdon,
Shall wedded be wi' me, wi' me,
Shall wedded be wi' me.

Then in there came young Breadalbane
Wi' a pistol on each side,
Come awa' Eppie Morrie
And I'll mak' you my bride, my bride,
And I'll mak' you my bride.

Go, get me a horse, Willie,
And get it like a man,
And send me back to my mither,
A maiden as I cam', I cam',
A maiden as I cam'.

The sun shines on the westlin hills
By the lamplicht of the moon,
Come, saddle your horse, young John Forsythe,
And whistle and I'll come soon, come soon,
Whistle and I'll come soon.

TAIL TODDLE

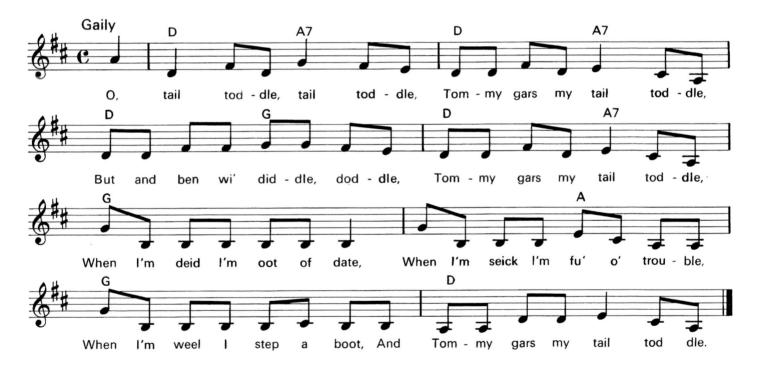

Gaily

O, tail tod-dle, tail tod-dle, Tom-my gars my tail tod-dle,

But and ben wi' did-dle, dod-dle, Tom-my gars my tail tod-dle,

When I'm deid I'm oot of date, When I'm seick I'm fu' o' trou-ble,

When I'm weel I step a boot, And Tom-my gars my tail tod dle.

O tail toddle, tail toddle,
Tommy gars my tail toddle,
But an ben wi' diddle doddle,
Tommy gars my tail toddle.

When I'm deid I'm oot of date,
When I'm seik I'm fu' o' trouble,
When I'm weel I step aboot,
And Tommy gars my tail toddle.

Jessie Mack, she gied a plack,
Helen Wallace gied a boddle,
Said the bride, "That's ower little,"
For to mend a broken doddle.

Oor guid wife held ower to Fife
For to buy a coal-riddle,
Lang ere she cam' back again,
Tommy made my tail toddle.

THE WIND BLEW THE BONNIE LASSIE'S PLAIDIE AWA'

Gaily

There was a bon-nie las - sie and she cam' in frae Crieff, she met up wi' a but-cher lad when he was sell-ing beef: The beef was in her bas-ket and she could-na rise a - wa And the wind blew the bon-nie las-sie's plaid - ie a - wa'. The wind blows east and the wind blows west and the wind blew the bon-nie las-sie's plaid - ie a - wa'. The

There was a bonnie lassie and she cam' in frae Crieff,
She met up wi' a butcher lad when he was selling beef;
He gied to her a belly-cut and doon she did fa'
And the wind blew the bonnie lassie's plaidie awa'.
    The wind blows East and the wind blows West,
    And the wind blew the bonnie lassie's plaidie
      awa'.
    And the wind blew the bonnie lassie's plaidie
      awa'.

The plaidie was lost and it couldna' be found
And the lassie and the butcher lad were lying on the
    ground
"O whit will I say to the auld folks ava?"
"For a darena' say the wind blew my plaidie awa'"
    The wind blows . . .
    He's gi'en her good measure o' the beef and
      banes and a'
    And the wind blew . . .

Twa-three months after the plaidie it was lost,
The lassie she began to swell aboot the waist;
The Rab he was blamed for the whole o' it a',
And the wind blawin' the bonnie lassie's plaidie awa'
    The lassie cried "Your butcher beef is over
      touch to chaw!"

Then Rab he was summoned to appear before the
    session,
And ane and a' cried oot, "Ye maun mak' a
    confession,"
But Rab never answered them ae word at a'
But, "The wind blew the bonnie lassie's plaidie awa'"
    We both fell to admiring for the beef it was
      sae braw.

The auld wife she cam' in the laddie to accuse,
The minister and elders began to abuse
The butcher lad for tryin' to make ane into twa,
But Rab said, "The wind blew the plaidie awa'."
    The lassie she was carryin' the beef, it wasna
        sma'.

The lassie she was sent for to come there hersel'
She looked at the butcher lad, "Ye ken hoo I feel,
The beef was the cause o't, ye daurna say na',
For 'twas then that the wind blew my plaidie awa'."
    The beef it was sae fresh that it wouldna keep
        at a'.

Rab lookit at the lassie and he gied a wee smile.
He said, "Bonnie lassie, I winna you beguile,
The minister he' here and he'll mak' ane o' us twa,
That will pay for the plaid that the wind blew awa'."
    The wind blows east and the wind blows west,
    The wind blew the bonnie lassie's plaidie awa',
    And we shall hae the middle cut, it's tenderest
        o' a'.
    And we'll drink tae the wind that blew your
        plaidie awa'!

WHO WILL MOW ME NOW?

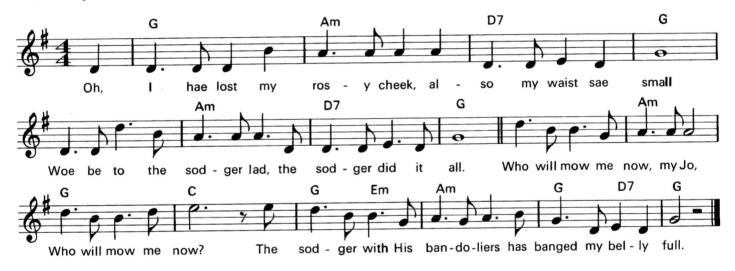

Oh, I hae lost my rosy cheek,
Also my waist sae small,
Woe be to the Sodger lad,
The sodger did it all.
    Who will mow me now, my Jo,
    Who will mow me now.
    A sodger with his bandoliers
    Has banged my belly full.

For I maun bear the scornful sneer
Of many a saucy queen,
When, curses on her godly face
Her gate's as merry as mine.

Our dame holds up her wanton tail
As oft as she down lies.
And yet will slander a young thing
If she the trade but tries.

Our dame has got her ain good man
And loves for glutton greed,
And yet will slander a poor thing
Wha loves but for its bread.

Alack so sweet a tree as love
Such bitter fruit should bear.
Alas that ever a merry part
Should draw so many a tear.

THE CUCKOO'S NEST

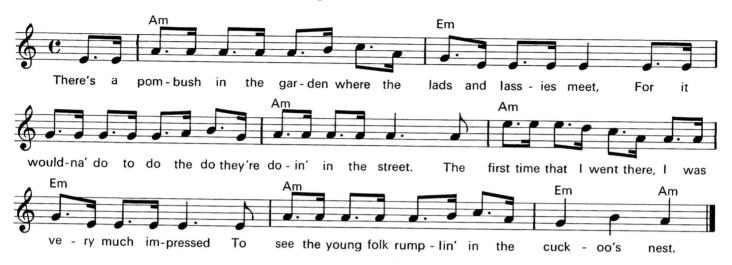

There's a pom-bush in the gar-den where the lads and lass-ies meet, For it would-na' do to do the do they're do-in' in the street. The first time that I went there, I was ve-ry much im-pressed To see the young folk rump-lin' in the cuck-oo's nest.

There's a pombush in the garden where the lads and lassies meet,
For it wouldna' do to do the do there doin' in the street;
The first time that I went there I was very much impressed
To see the young folks rumplin' in the cuckoo's nest.

It's hi! the cuckin' ho! the cuckin'
Hi! the cuckoo's nest,
Hi! the cuckin' ho! the cuckin'
Hi! the cuckoo's nest;
I'll give any man a shilling and a bottle of the best
Who'll rumple up the feathers of the cuckoo's nest.

I met her in the mornin' and I had her in the night;
I'd never gone that way before and had to do it right.
I never would have found it and I never would have guessed
If she hadn't showed me where to find the cuckoo's nest.

She showed me where to find it and she showed me where to go
Through the prickles and the brambles where the little cuckoos grow;
From the moment that I found it she would never let me rest
'Till I'd rumpled up the feathers of the cuckoo's nest.

It was thorny, it was prickled, it was feathered all around,
It was tucked into a corner where it wasn't easy found,
She said, "Young man, you're blundering," I said it wasn't true;
I left her with the makin's of a young cuckoo.

JOHN ANDERSON, MY JO

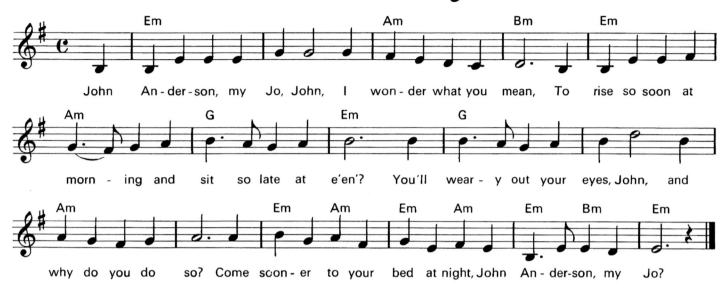

John An-der-son, my Jo, John, I won-der what you mean, To rise so soon at morn-ing and sit so late at e'en? You'll wear-y out your eyes, John, and why do you do so? Come soon-er to your bed at night, John An-der-son, my Jo?

John Anderson, my Jo, John, I wonder what you mean,
To rise so soon at the morning and sit so late at e'en?
You'll weary out your eyes, John, and why do you do so?
Come sooner to your bed at night,
John Anderson, my Jo.

John Anderson, my friend John, when you first in life began,
You had as good a tail tree as any other man,
But now 'tis waxing old, John, and waggles to and fro,
And never stands alone now,
John Anderson, my jo.

John Anderson, my jo, John, you can love where e'er you please,
Either in our warm bed, or else aboon the clothes,
Or you shall have the horns, John, upon your head to grow,
For that was always the cuckold's curse,
John Anderson, my jo.

So when you want to have me, John, see that you do your best,
And when you begin to kiss me see that you hold me fast,
See that you grip me fast, John, until that I cry "Oh!"
Your back shall crack, ere I cry, "Slack!"
John Anderson, my jo.

Oh, but it is a fine thing to peek out o'er the fence,
But 'tis a far, far finer thing to see your back commence;
To see your back commence, John, to wriggle to and fro,
'Tis then I like your changer pipe,
John Anderson, my jo.

I'm backit like a salmon, I'm breasted like a swan,
My belly is a down sack, my middle you may span,
From my crown until my toe, John, I'm like the new fallen snow,
And 'tis all for your conveniency,
John Anderson, my jo.

THE COOPER OF DUNDEE

You Coopers and Hoopers attend to my ditty
I'll tell of a man who dwelt in Dundee,
This young man he was both am'rous and witty,
He pleased the fair maids wi' a blink of his ee.

He wasna a cooper, a common tub hooper,
The most of his trade lay in pleasing the fair,
He hooped them, he cooped them, he bored them,
   he plugged them,
And all sent for Sandy when oot of repair.

For a twelvemonth or so this youth was respected,
And he was as busy as well he might be,
But business increased so that some were neglected
Which ruined his trade in the town of Dundee.

Now a bailiff's daughter had wanted a cooping,
And Sandy was sent for as often was he,
He yerkt her sae hard that she sprung her end hooping,
Which banished poor Sandy from bonnie Dundee.

WE'RE A' JOLLY FU'

Saw a loose chase a moose,
Wha's fu, Wha's fu'?
Saw a loose chase a moose
Roond the riggin l' a hoose,
And we're a' blin' drunk, Jolly fu!

Saw an eel chase the deil
Roond and roond a tattie field.

Saw a snail chase a whale
Roond aboot a parritch pail.

Saw a bug chase a dog
Up and down the old wife's leg.

Saw a puggie chase a cuddie
Roond aboot a lassie's bubbie.

Saw a flea runnin' free
Up and doon a stream of pee.

Saw a knife chase a wife
And cut the man a muckle slice.

GREEN GROW THE RASHES

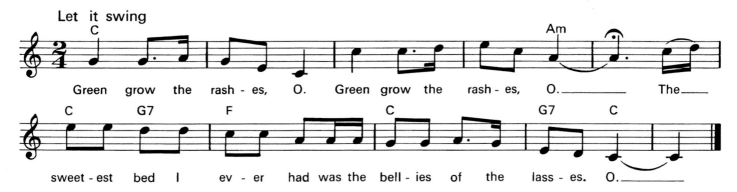

Let it swing

Green grow the rash - es, O. Green grow the rash - es, O._____ The_____

sweet - est bed I ev - er had was the bell - ies of the lass - es. O._____

Green grow the rashes o,
Green grow the rashes o,
The sweetest bed I ever had
Was the bellies of the lasses, o.

Green grow the rashes, o,
Green grow the rashes, o,
The maidens they have luscious lips,
The widows they have gashes, o.

There's a pious lass in town,
Godly Lizzie Lundy, o,
She mounts the peak throughout the week
But fingers it on Sunday, o.

Lizzie is of large dimension,
There is not a doubt of it,
The soccer team went in last night,
And none has yet come out of it.

Jickie's wife she thought she'd shave it,
Threw him in a pretty passion,
Shouting he'd not have a wife
Whose private parts were out of fashion.

We're all full from eating of it,
We're all dry from drinking of it,
The parson kissed the fiddler's wife
And could not preach for thinking of it.

Green grow the rashes, o
Green grow the rashes, o
A feather bed is nae sae soft
As the bellies of the lasses, o.

THE KEACH IN THE CREEL

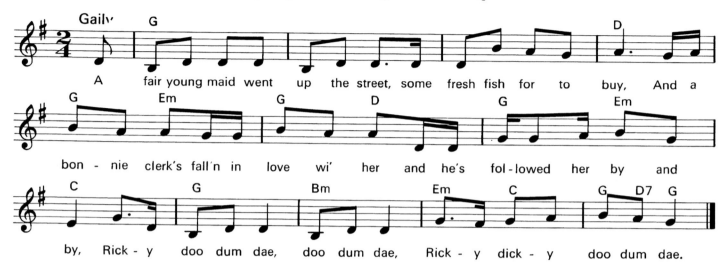

A fair young maid went up the street, some fresh fish for to buy, And a bon - nie clerk's fall'n in love wi' her and he's fol - lowed her by and by, Rick - y doo dum dae, doo dum dae, Rick - y dick - y doo dum dae.

A fair young maid went up the street
Some fresh fish for to buy,
And a bonnie clerk's fall'n in love wi' her
And he's followed her by and by.
    Ricky doo dum dae, doo dum dae,
    Ricky dicky doo dum dae.

"My faither he aye licks the door
And my mither keeps the key,
And though the nicht were never sae mirk,
Ye couldna win in tae me."

Now the clerk he had a true brother,
And a wily wicht was he,
And he has made a lang ladder
Wi' thirty steps and three.

He has made a pin but and a creel,
A creel but and a pin,
And he has gone to the chimla-top
To let the bonnie clerk in.

Now the old wife she lie wide awake
Though late, late was the hour;
"I'll lie my life," said the silly old wife,
"There's a man in our dochter's bower."

The old man he gat oot o' the bed
To see gin the thing was true;
But she's ta'en the bonnie clerk in her arms
And covered him over with blue.

"What are ye daeing, my ain dochter?
What are ye daein', my doo?"
"I'm praying on the muckle buik
For my silly old mammie and you."

"Pray on, pray on, my ain dochter,
And see that ye do it richt,
If ever a woman has tint her reason
Your mither has done this nicht."

"O wife, o wife, ye silly old wife,
An ill deith may ye dee;
She's gotten the muckly buil in her arms
An' she's praying for you and me."

The old wife she lay wide awake,
No' anither word was said,
Till, "I'll lay my life," said the silly old wife,
"There's a man in our dochter's bed."

"Get up again, my old guid man,
And see gin the thing be true."
"Get up yoursel' ye silly old wife
I'll no be fashed wi' you."

"Get up yoursel' ye silly old wife,
And may the feil tak' ye,
For atween you and your ae dochter,
I havna aince blinkit an ee."

The old wife she gat oower the bed
To see gin the thing be true,
But she slippit her fit and fell into the creel,
And up the tow he drew.

"Oh help, oh help, my old guid man!
O help me noo, my doo!
For he that ye wished me wi' this nicht,
I fear he's gotten me noo."

The man that was at the chimla top
Finding the creel was fu',
He wrapt the rope his shoulder roond
And up the two he drew.

"Gin he has got ye, I wish he may haud ye,
I wish he may haud ye fast,
For atween you and your ae dochter
I hanna aince gotten my rest."

Oh, he the blue and the bonnie bonnie blue,
And I wish the blue richt weel,
And for ilka old wife that wakes at nicht,
May she get a guid keach in the creel.

NINE INCH WILL PLEASE A LADY

Come tell me, dame, Come tell me, dame, My dame come tell me tru____
What length of tool, when used by rule will serve a maid-en du - ly. The
auld___ dame clawed her wan - ton tail, Her wan - ton tail sae read - y. I
learned__ a song in An - nan-dale, Nine inch will please a la - dy.

"Come tell me dame, come tell me dame,
My dame come tell me truly,
What length of tool when used by rule,
Will serve a woman duly?"
The auld dame clawed her wanton tail,
Her wanton tail sae ready,
"I learned a song in Annandale,
'Nine inch will please a lady'.

"But for a country cage like mine,
In sooth we're not sae gentle;
We'll take two thumb-widths to the nine,
And that is a jolly pintle.
Oh, blessings on me Charlie lad,
I'll ne'er forget me Charlie,
Two roaring handfuls and good bit more,
He nudged it in full rarely.

"But woe be to the lazy rump
And may it ne'er be thriving,
It's not the length that makes me jump,
But it's the double driving.
Come nidge me, Tom, come nidge me, Tom.
Come nidge me, do it straightway,
Come loosen free your battering ram
And bang him away at my gateway.

Nine inch will please a lady."

LASSIE GATHERING NUTS

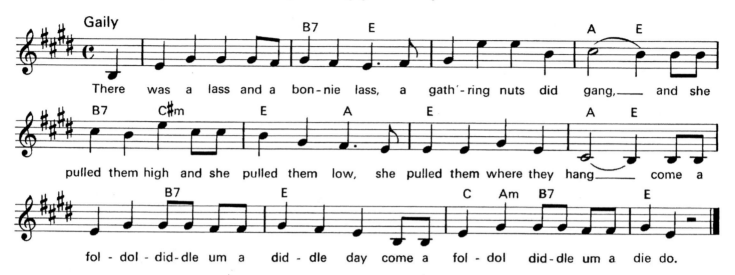

There was a lass and a bonnie lass, a gath'-ring nuts did gang,___ and she pulled them high and she pulled them low, she pulled them where they hang___ come a fol - dol - did-dle um a did - dle day come a fol - dol did-dle um a die do.

There was a lass and a bonnie lass,
A-gathering nuts did gang,
And she pulled them high and she pulled them low,
And she pulled them where they hang.
　　Come a fol-dol-diddle um a diddle day,
　　Come a fol-dol-diddle um a di-do.

Till tired at length she laid her doon,
And slept the woods among,
When by there came three lusty lads,
Three lusty lads and strong.

Oh, the first did kiss her rosy lips,
He thought it wasna' wrong,
The second unloosened her bodice fair
That was sewed wi' silk along.

And what the third did to the lass
Is no put in this song,
But the lassie wakened in a fright
And she says, "I have slept too long."

DUNCAN MACLEERIE

Dun-can Mac - Leer - ie and Jan - et his wife, went to the fair____ to
buy a new knife. But in - stead of a knife they just danced them-selves
wear - y "We're ver - y well served, Jan," said Dun - can Mac - Leer - ie.

Duncan Macleerie and Janet his wife,
They went to the fair to buy a new knife,
But instead of a knife they just danced themselves
    weary.
"We're very well served, Jan," says Duncan Macleerie.

Duncan Macleerie has got a new fiddle,
All strung with hair with a hole in the middle,
And when he plays on it his wife looks so cheery.
"Well done my Duncan," said Janet Macleerie.

Duncan he played till his bow it got greasy,
Janet grew fretful and uncommon uneasy.
"Hoot," says she, "Duncan, you're very soon weary;
Play us a tune," says Janet Macleerie.

Duncan Macleerie he played on the harp,
Janet Macleerie she danced in her sark,
Her sark it was short and her legs they were hairy,
"Very well danced, Jan," says Duncan Macleerie.

THE PATRIARCH

Tune: "Lassie Gathering Nuts"

As Honest Jacob on a nicht
Wi' his beloved beauty,
Was duly laid in wedlock's bed
But nodding at his duty.
 Come a fol-dol-diddle um-a-diddle day,
 Come a fol-dol-diddle um-a-diddle.

"How long," she cried, "You fumbling wretch,
Will you be at it jigging?
My oldest child might die of age
Before you do your digging.

"You puff and groan and goggle there
And you make uncommon splutter,
And I must lie and suffer you
Though I'm not a hair the better."

Then he in wrath put up his scythe,
"The devil's in this huzzie;
Why I mow you as I mow the rest,
By night and day I'm busy.

"I've got wi' child our servants both
And by your titty, Rachel,
You barren jade, you drive me mad,
For all, you're still ungrateful.

"There's never a mow I've given the rest
But what you've had a dozen,
But not a one you'll get again,
Even though your gate turn frozen."

Then Rachel calm as any lamb,
She puts him on her belly,
She says, "What matter a woman's chatter,
In truth you mow me jolly."

"My dear, 'tis so for many a mow
I am your grateful debtor,
But once again I think and then
You'll maybe find it better."

The honest man wi' little work,
He soon forgot his ire,
The Patriarch threw off his shirt
And up and at it like fire.

Songs of the Auld Sod

By contrast with the earthy humor that pervades Scot's songs, the songs of Ireland are made of sterner stuff. From 1169 England's first invasion through the ill-fated Fenian rebellion of the 1860's and even to the present civil war in Northern Ireland, the Auld Sod has been a land torn by war and rebellion. English against Irish, Protestant against Catholic, with only a drink to raise the heart in a man. It is small wonder that most of Ireland's songs are of heroes and whiskey, some of the best of which have been collected by the Clancy Brothers and Tommy Makem. As for the rest, even when songs of wenching were sung, the hero most likely got caught with his pants down or with a case of the clap.

The Sergeant

The melody of this undoubtedly came from some delicate English madrigal. The words didn't.

(*1, 11, 17-I*)

The Limerick Rake

This ballad is probably of the late 18th century. The towns mentioned identify it as a Munster song, most of them being in Limerick County. The classical references are typical of many Irish ballads of this period, and show the hand of the "hedge schoolmaster." The last line of each verse, "agus fagaimid siud mar atase" (pronounced: agus fa ga mid schood mar a ta say), is Gaelic, and means "and we leave them as we found them." (*6*)

A Quick Way to Be Rid of a Wife (*21*)

The Unfortunate Rake

This homilectic ballad of a soldier who dies of syphilis has been the father of a widespread family of ballads and songs, including among them the well-known "Cowboy's Lament" and "Gambler's Blues." It was spread far and wide by the 19th century ballad presses, and quickly developed many variants—"The Trooper Cut Down in His Prime," "The St. James Hospital," often collected in America as "The Bad Girls Lament," the sex of the victim was changed and it became the story of unfortunate prostitute dying of venereal disease. Elsewhere in America, it was taken up by the Negroes of New Orleans and became a jazz standby as "St. James Infirmary" or "Gambler's Blues." It was carried to the West, where the hero died a more heroic death from gunshot wounds, and to the North where the hero, a lineman, fell off a telephone pole to his doom. In all these, though, the original ballad is easily recognized; the dying man requests a military burial complete with fife and drums, and guns to be fired over his coffin. As he is lowered to his grave, he warns the onlookers of the dangers of following his bad example. This version is probably quite close to the original. The St. James Hospital was a real hospital in London, and is now the site of the Court of St. James. Salts of white mercury were administered to cure syphilis. (*23*)

Lillibullero

Burnet, a historian contemporary with the event, wrote: "A foolish ballad was made at that time, treating the Papists, and chiefly the Irish, in a very ridiculous manner, which had a burden said to be Irish words, 'Lero, lero, lilliburler', that made an impression on the (King's) army, that cannot be imagined by those who saw it not. The whole army, and at last the people, both in city and country, were singing it perpetually. And perhaps never had so slight a thing had so great an effect."

The song was written by Lord Wharton, a viceroy of Ireland, who boasted later that he had "whistled a king out of three kingdoms." It was written on the Earl of Tyrconnel's appointment to the lieutenantcy of Ireland by King James II. He had, according to Percy, "recommended himself to his bigoted master by his arbitrary treatment of the Protestants in the preceding year." "Lillibullero" and "bullen a-la" were reportedly passwords used by the Irish Catholics in their massacre of the Protestants in 1641. The tune is a harpsichord exercise written earlier by Purcell which had passed into oral tradition to become a well-known jig-tune. It has been used since for "The Protestant Boys." (*6, 13*)

I've Got a Sister Lilly

This song was learned in Chicago, 1961, from an amateur folklorist who collected it in 1959 from a student who learned it from a Scots plumber who had learned it in London. Since then we have located an English student who claimed to know it but refused to sing it.

The Chandler's Wife (*11, 17-I*)

THE SERGEANT

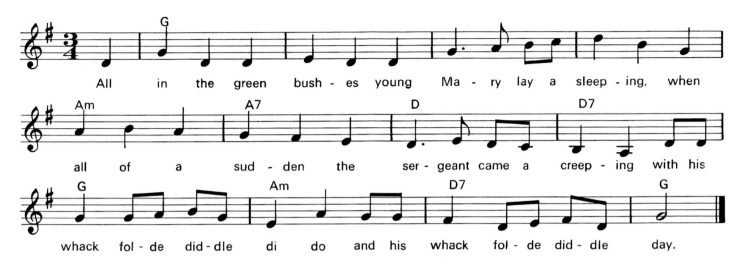

All in the green bush-es young Ma-ry lay a sleep-ing, when all of a sud-den the ser-geant came a creep-ing with his whack fol-de did-dle di do and his whack fol-de did-dle day.

All in the green bushes young Mary lay a-sleeping
When all of a sudden the Sergeant came a-creeping,
    With his whack-fol-de-diddle di do
    And his whack-fol-di-diddle day.

A few months went by and young Mary she grew
    bolder
And wished that the Sergeant would come and do
    it over.

A few months went by and young Mary she grew
    fatter
And all of the neighbors were wondering who'd been
    at her.

A few months went by and young Mary burst
    asunder,
And out popped a little sergeant with a regimental
    number.

New words & music by Oscar Brand.
©Copyright 1950, 1960 Oscar Brand, New York. Used by permission.

THE LIMERICK RAKE

I am a young fellow that's easy and bold, In Castle-town Conner's I'm very well known, In New-Castle west I spent many a note with Kitty and Judy and Mary My father rebuked me for being such a rake, and spending me time in such frolic-some ways, but I ne'er could for-get the good na-ture of Jane, ag-us fa' gaim id siud mar a - ta se.

I am a young fellow that's easy and bold,
In Castletown Connors I'm very well known,
In Newcastle West I spent many a note
With Kitty and Judy and Mary.
My father rebuked me for being such a rake
And for spending my time in such frolicsome ways,
But I ne'er could forget the good nature of Jane,
Agus fagaimid siud mar atase.

My parents had reared me to shake and to mow,
To plow and to harrow, to reap and to sow
But my heart being too airy to drop it so low
I set out on high speculation.
On paper and parchment they taught me to write
In Euclid and grammar they opened my eyes,
In multiplication in truth I was bright,
Agus fagaimid siud mar atase.

If I chance for to go to the town of Rathkeal
The women all round me do gather and stare,
Some bring me a bottle and others sweet cakes
And I kiss them unknown to their parents.
There is one from Askeaton and one from the Pike
Another from Arda has my heart beguiled
Though being from the mountains her stockings are
    white
Agus fagaimid siud mar atase.

To quarret for riches I ne'er was inclined
For the greatest of misers must leave 'em behind
So I'll purchase a cow which will never run dry
And I'll milk her by twisting her horn.
John Damer of Shronel had plenty of gold
And Devonshire's treasure is twenty times more
But they're laid on their backs among nettles and
    stones
Agus fagaimid siud mar atase.

If I chance for to go to the market at Croom
With a cock in my hat and my pipes in full tune
I am welcomed at once and brought up to a room
Where Bacchus is sporting with Venus.
There's Peggy and Jane from the town of Bruree
And Biddy from Bruff and we're all on a spree
Such a combing of licks as there was about me,
Agus fagaimid siud mar atase.

There's some says I'm foolish and more says I'm wise
But being fond of the women I think is no crime
For the son of King David had ten hundred wives
And His wisdom was highly regarded.
I'll till a good garden and live at my ease
Each woman and child can partake of the same
If there's war in the cabin, themselves they may blame
Agus fagaimid siud mar atase.

And now for the future I mean to be wise
And I'll send for the women who've acted so kind
And I'll marry them all on the morrow by and by
If the clergy agree to the bargain.
And when I'm on my back and my soul is at peace
These women will crowd for to cry at my wake
And their sons and their daughters can offer their
    prayers
To the Lord for the soul of their fathers.

A QUICK WAY TO BE RID OF A WIFE

I had a wife and got no good of her, Tell ye how I ea-sy got rid of her:
Took her out and chopped the head of her, Ear - lie in the morn - ing.

I had a wife and got no good of her
Here is how I easy got rid of her
Took her out and chopped the head of her
Early in the morning.

Seeing as how there was no evidence
For the sheriff or his reverence
They had to call it an act of providence
Early in the morning.

So if you've a wife and get no good of her
Here is how to easy get rid of her
Take her out and chop the head of her
Early in the morning.

THE UNFORTUNATE RAKE

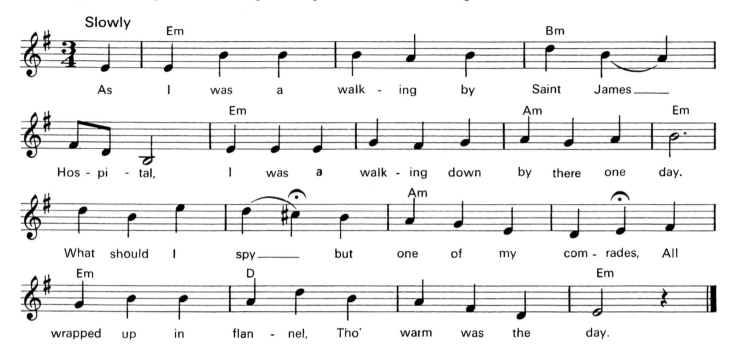

As I was a-walking down by St. James' hospital
I was a-walking down by there one day
What should I spy but one of my comerades
All wrapped up in flannel tho warm was the day.

I asked him what ailed him I asked him what failed him
I asked the cause of all his complaint.
"It's all on account of some handsome young woman,
'Tis she that has caused me to weep and lament.

"And had she but told me before she disordered me,
Had she but told me of it in time
I might have got pills and salts of white mercury
But now I'm cut down in the height of my prime.

"Get six young soldiers to carry my coffin
Six young girls to sing me a song,
And each of them carry a bunch of green laurel
So they don't smell me as they bear me along.

"Don't muffle your drums and play your fifes merrily
Play a quick march as you carry me along
Fire your bright muskets all over my coffin
Saying, 'There goes an unfortunate lad to his home'."

50

LILLIBULLERO

Ho, Bro-ther Teaque, dost hear the de-cree Lil-li-bul-le-ro bul-len-a-la

That we shall have a new De-pu-ty Lil-li-bul-le-ro bul-len-a-la

le-ro le-ro lil-li bul-le-ro lil-li bul-le-ro bul-len-a-la

le-ro le-ro lil-li bul-le-ro lil-li bul-le-ro bul-len-a-la.

Ho brother Teague, dost hear the decree
Lillibullero bullen a la
Dat we shall have a new Deputy
Lillibullero bullen a la.
    Lero, lero, lillibullero
    Lillibullero, bullen a la,
    Lero' lero, lillibullero
    Lillibullero, bullen a la.

Ho, by my Soul, it is a Talbot,
And he will cut all the English Throat.

Though, by my Soul, di English do prate,
De Law's on dere side and Christ knows what.

But if Dispence do come from the Pope
We'll hang Magna Cart and demselves in a rope.

And the good Talbot is now made a lord
And with his brave lads he's coming aboard.

Who in all France have taken a swear,
Dat day will have no Protestant heir.

O but why does he stay behind?
Ho by my Soul, 'tis a Protestant wind.

Now that Tyrconnel is come ashore
And we shall have commissions go leor.

And he dat will not go to the Mass
Shall be turned out, and look like an ass.

Now, now de hereticks all will go down
By Christ and Saint Patrick the nation's our own.

There was an old prophecy found in a bog
That Ireland be ruled by an ass and a dog.

This prophecy now is come to pass
For Talbot's the dog, and James is the ass.

51

I'VE GOT A SISTER LILLY

I've got a sister Lilly, she's a whore in Picadilly
And my mother runs a brothel on the Strand
Me father cocks his asshole at the guards of Windsor
    Castle
We're a filthy, fucking family but we're grand.

Oh, please don't burn our shit-house down,
Mother has promised to pay,
Dad's laid up with the old D.T.'s
And the cat's in a family way.

Brother's been caught peddling morphine,
Sister's been hustling so hard,
Sof if you burn our shit-house down,
We'll have to make do with the yard.

THE CHANDLER'S WIFE

A man walked into a chandler's shop, some candles for to buy,
And when he got into the shop nobody did he spy,
When he turned upon his heels and toward the door he sped,
When he heard the sound of a (***), right above his head,
Yes, he heard the sound of a (***), right above his head.

Now, this young man was a bold young man, so up the stairs he sped,
And very surprised was he to find the chandler's wife in bed,
And with her was a fine young man of very considerable size,
And they were having a (***) right before his eyes. *(repeat)*

Now when the fun was over and done she lifted up her head,
And very surprised was she to find the man beside her bed,
"If you will keep my secret, sir, if you will be so kind,
You may drop in for a (***) whenever you feel inclined. *(repeat)*

So, all you married men take heed, if ever you come to town,
If you must leave your woman at home, be sure to tie her down,
Or, if you would be kind to her, just sit her down on the floor,
And give her so much of that (***) she doesn't need any more. *(repeat)*

New words & New music adaptation by Oscar Brand.

BLOW, BOYS, BLOW

This section contains two types of songs: shanties—the work-songs used aboard sailing ships, and forebitters, or fo'c's'le songs—ballads and songs which were sung by the sailors off duty. The sailor's quarters were called the forecastle, giving rise to the name. The forebitters were quite often shore songs which were thinly disguised or entirely unchanged. One characteristic which marks them is a complete lack of that drawing-room sentiment which comes down to us in songs about the jolly English tar with the heart of oak. The sailors themselves were rough, brutal men, at sea for months at a time with no women and only a cursing bucko mate to remind them of civilization. They themselves wouldn't have been welcome in a drawing room—so it is not surprising that drawing-room songs were unwelcome with them. All the forebitters presented below are on the record, *Blow, Boys, Blow* by A. L. Lloyd and Ewan MacColl.

The Handsome Cabin Boy

This song was circulated throughout the British Isles as a broadside in the 19th century, and was by no means confined to the open seas. So far as is known to the editors, it was not based on any particular incident, though the story is believable and certainly could have happened. The device of dressing a girl up in men's clothing is very old, having such distinguished ancestors as Jonson and Shakespeare; this is the most convincing story of the lot. The tune is quite daring for a folksong. If you prefer a bit of a faster tune, another, which was also used for this song, is given under the title, "The Butcher and the Tailor's Wife."

Cruising 'Round Yarmouth

A member of the "Ratcliff Highway" and "Blow the Man Down" family, this song uses the line, "She was round in the counter and bluff in the bow," which must occur in a hundred songs, and a better line could not be desired. A ship and its fittings is admirably suited for describing a woman—after all, a ship is always called "She." The melody is in 3/4 time, a rhythm almost universal among sea songs, which seems to give a feeling of the rolling of the waves, among other things.

The great days of the sea shanty were in the first sixty years of the 19th century, when the fast clipper ships were running. There was keen rivalry between the merchant companies, and the skippers of these ships were expected to drive their men to get the last knot out of their craft. "If the man don't sing right, the ship don't move right" was the saying, and a good shantyman was never in need of a job on a fast packet.

The shantyman would usually be hired just as a regular seaman, and when the ship was clearing the bar on its way to the sea, and the sailors were hauling on the halliards to raise more sail, the mate would holler, "Aye, you lazy lubbers, who's the nightingale on this here trip?" and one of the sailors with a good strong voice would strike up a shanty, usually singing the chorus first so that the men would know which shanty it was, and thereafter singing only the solo parts. He was expected to do his share of the work, but would usually take it a little easy on the heavy hauling to save his breath for the more important job of singing.

Roughly, shanties divide themselves into three kinds: capstan shanties—used at the capstan to weigh anchor, halliard shanties—for hoisting the heavy sails, and short drag shanties—for taking in slack or hauling on sheets and braces. While most shanties would fall into one of these three types, they could be interchanged, and a pumping or halliard shanty might find occasional use at the capstan or for a short drag.

The amount of improvisation allowed the shantyman varied with the shanty. The "White" shanties usually had enough standard verses to get through with the job at hand. If the shantyman ran out of verses, or his memory failed him, he would then improvise enough to carry him through. However, on the "Negro" shanties, only the first two or three verses were set, and the rest would be strictly improvised. Many a shantyman with a cracked, weak voice was kept on merely because of his ability to improvise filthy verses.

A Hundred Years

This halliard shanty evolved from a nineteenth century minstrel song, "A Long Time Ago."

(5)

Do Me Ama

Sailors loved to sing of their conquests and defeats ashore. The theme of the "jolly Jack tar" who outwits the squire and takes his woman was a favorite in many fo'c's'les. This particular song derives its story from the old chapbook tale, "The Squire and the Farm Servant." It is still current in Southeast England. The melody sounds like an attempt by the sailor to imitate some of the melodies heard at his Mediterranean ports of call.

Whup Jamboree

This wild shanty was mainly used at the capstan on the last part of the voyage, when the ship was almost ready to dock in its home port. The sequence of places mentioned describes an Indiaman docking at Liverpool. The gloriously unprintable last line of each verse is invariably bowdlerized when printed. We followed that practice ourselves, and took the line from *Shanties of the Seven Seas*, by Stan Hugill, who claims to have come closest to the original. (4)

Little Sally Racket

Seamen sang this at the tops'l halliards; it was said to be so very British that it was "frowned upon aboard American ships." This seems strange since the melody has a distinctly Negro ring to it, and probably derives from the Jamaican song, "Missy Ramsgate."

THE HANDSOME CABIN BOY

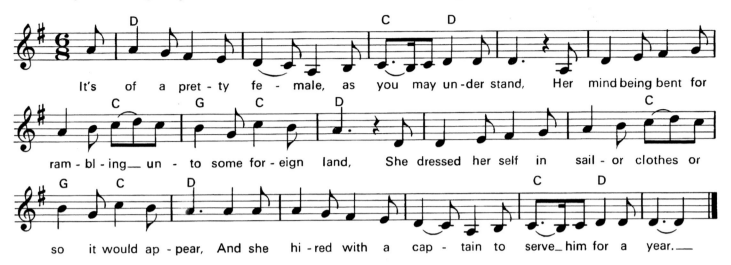

It's of a pretty female, as you may understand,
Her mind being bent for rambling unto some foreign land,
She dressed herself in sailor clothes, or so it does appear,
And hired with a captain to serve him for a year.

The captain's wife, she being on board, she seemed in great joy
To think her husband had engaged such a handsome cabin boy,
And now and then she'd slip him a kiss and she would have liked to toy,
But it was the captain found out the secret of the handsome cabin boy.

Her cheeks they were like roses and her hair all in a curl,
The sailors often smiled and said, "He looks just like a girl."
But eating of the captain's biscuits their color did destroy
And the waist did swell of pretty Nell, the handsome cabin boy.

It was in the Bay of Biscay our gallant ship did plow.
One night among our sailors was a fearful flurry and row.
They tumbled from their hammocks for their sleep it did destroy
And they swore about the groaning of the handsome cabin boy.

"Oh doctor, oh doctor," the cabin boy did cry,
"My time is come, I am undone, and I shall surely die."
The doctor come around in a-smiling and in fun
To think a sailor lad could have a daughter or a son.

The sailors, when they saw the joke, they did all stand and stare.
The child belonged to none of them they solemnly did swear.
The captain's wife she said to him, "My dear, I wish you joy,
For it's either you or I has betrayed the handsome cabin boy."

So each man took his tot of rum and drank success to trade,
And likewise to the cabin boy who was neither man nor maid.
Here's hoping that the wars don't rise, our sailors to destroy,
And here's hoping for a jolly lot more like the handsome cabin boy.

CRUISING 'ROUND YARMOUTH

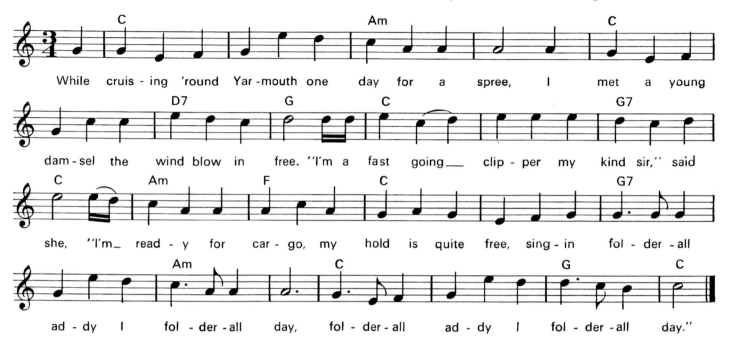

While cruis-ing 'round Yar-mouth one day for a spree, I met a young dam-sel the wind blow in free. "I'm a fast going____ clip-per my kind sir," said she, "I'm____ read-y for car-go, my hold is quite free, sing-in fol-der-all ad-dy I fol-der-all day, fol-der-all ad-dy I fol-der-all day."

While cruising round Yarmouth one day for a spree
I met a fair damsel, the wind blowing free,
"I'm a fast-going clipper, my king sir," said she,
"I'm ready for cargo, my hold is quite free."
    Singing fol der all addy I fol der all day,
    Fol der all addy, I fol der all day.

What country she came from I could not tell which.
By her appearance I thought she was Dutch.
Her flag wore its colors, her masthead was low,
She was round in the counter and bluff in the bow.

I gave her the rope and I took her in tow,
Yardarm to yardarm a-towing we go.
We both towed together till we came to the quay,
We both towed together through Trafalgary Bay.

She took me upstairs and her tops'l she lowered,
In a neat little landing she soon had me moored.
She lowered her fores'ls, her stays'ls and all,
With her lily white hand on me reef-tackle fall.

I said, "Pretty fair maid, it's time to give o'er,
For 'twixt wind and water ye've run me ashore.
My shot-locker's empty, me powder's all spent,
I can't fire a shot for I'm choked to the vent."

Here's luck to the girl who ran Jack on the rocks,
And here's to the girl with the black curly locks;
Here's luck to the doctor who eased all his pain,
He's squared his main yards, he's a-cruising again.

A HUNDRED YEARS

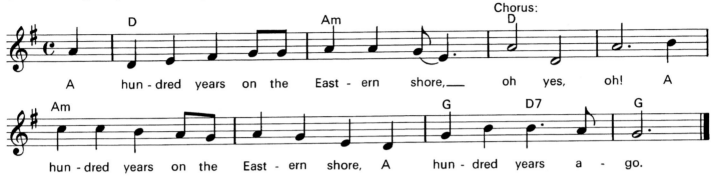

A hun-dred years on the East-ern shore,___ oh yes, oh! A hun-dred years on the East-ern shore, A hun-dred years a - go.

A hundred years on the Eastern shore,
Oh yes, oh!
A hundred years on the Eastern shore,
A hundred years ago!

When I sailed across the sea,
My gal said she'd be true to me.

I promised her a golden ring,
She promised me that little thing.

Oh, Bully John was the boy for me,
A bully on land and a Bucko at sea.

Ol' Bully John from Baltimore,
I knew him well, that son-of-a-whore.

Ol' Bully John, I knew him well,
But now he's dead an' gone to hell.

When I was young and in my prime
I'd knock those little gals two at a time.

It's up aloft this yeard must go.
For Mister Mate, he told us so.

I thought I heard the skipper say,
Just one more pull and then belay.

Note: Shanties are always sung unaccompanied.

Do Me Ama

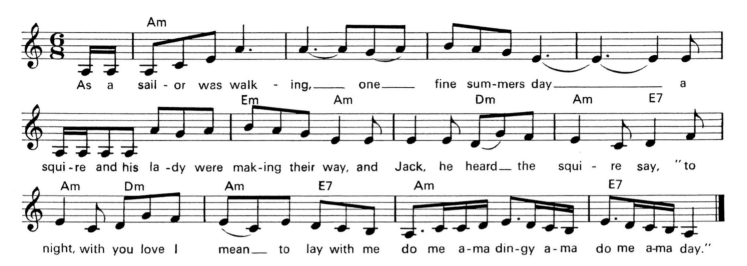

As a sail-or was walk - ing,____ one____ fine sum-mers day____ a
squi-re and his la -dy were mak-ing their way, and Jack, he heard__ the squi - re say, "to
night, with you love I mean__ to lay with me do me a-ma din-gy a-ma do me a-ma day."

As a sailor was walking one fine summer's day,
A squire and his lady were making their way,
And Jack, he heard the squire say,
"Tonight with you, love, I mean to lay,
With me do me ama ding-y ama, do me ama day."

"You must tie a string all around your finger
With the other end of the string hanging out the
　　window,
And I'll step by and I'll pull the string,
And you come down and you let me in"
With me do me ama, ding-y ama, do me ama day.

Says Jack to himself, "I've a mind to try,
To see if a poor sailor, he can't win that prize."
So he stepped by and he pulled the string
And the lady came down and she let him in
With his do me ama ding-y ama, do me ama day.

When the squire came by he was humming a song,
Thinking to himself how it would not be long.
But when he got there, no string he found,
Behold, his hopes all dashed to the ground
And his do me ama ding-y ama do me ama day.

Early next morning it was just getting light,
The lady woke up in a terrible fright.
There lay Jack in his stripey shirt,
His hands all covered with tar and dirt,
And his do me ama ding-y ama, do me ama day.

"Oh what do you want, you dirty sailor,
Breaking in a lady's bedroom to steal her treasure,"
"Oh, no," says old Jack, "I just pulled the string,
And you come down and you let me in,"
With me do me ama ding-y ama, do me ama day.

Says Jack to the lady, "Oh forgive me, I pray,
I'll steal away very quietly at the break of the day."
"Oh no," says the lady, "don't stray too far,
For I never shall part from my jolly Jack Tar
And his do me ama ding-y ama, do me ama day.

WHUP JAMBOREE

Now m'lads be of good cheer
For the Irish land will soon draw near,
In a few days more we'll sight cape Clear,
Ooh! Jinny, keep your ringtail warm.
    Whup Jamboree, Whup Jamboree,
    Ai-i-i! Y'ring tailed black man
    Sheet it home behind,
    Whup Jamboree, Whup Jamboree,
    Ooooh! Jinnie keep yer ringtail warm!

Now me boys, we're off Holyhead
An' there's no more casts of the dipsy lead,
Soon we'll be in a lovely fevver bed,
Ooooh! Jinnie keep yer ringtail warm.

Now the Barship is in sight,
An' soon we'll be off the ol' Rock Light,
An' I'll be cleaning out yer flue tonight,
Ooooh! Jinnie keep yer ringtail warm.

Now we're haulin' through the dock
All the pretty young gals on the pierhead do flock
An' there's my Jinnie in a new pink frock
Ooooh! Jinnie keep yer ringtail warm!

Now we're tied to the pier
Oh, it's way down below, an' pack yer musty gear,
An' I'll soon be a-kissin' o' you, me dear,
Ooooh! Jinnie keep yer ringtail warm.

Now I'm safe upon the shore,
An' I don't give a damn how the winds do roar,
For I'll drop me anchor an' I'll go to sea no more,
Ooooh! Jinnie keep yer ringtail warm.

But now I've had two weeks ashore,
I'll pack me bags an' I'll go t sea once more,
An' I'll bid goodbye to me Liverpool whore,
Ooooh! Jinnie keep yer ringtail warm.

LITTLE SALLY RACKET

Lit-tle Sal-ly Rack - et, Haul 'em a - way,___ She pawned my best jack-et, Haul 'em a-way, and she

lost the tick - et, Haul 'em a - way. So___ had it high - er, Haul 'em a - way.___

Little Sally Racket
Haul him away
She pawned my best jacket,
Haul him away,
And she lost the ticket,
Haul him away
So haul it higher
Haul him away.

Little Kitty Carson
Got up with a parson
Now she's got a little bar'son
So haul it higher.

Little Nancy Dawson
Well, she got a notion
For a poor old bo's'n
So haul it higher.

Little Susie Skinner,
She says she's a beginner,
She prefers it to a dinner,
So up lads and in her.

Well, my fighting cocks, boys,
Haul and split the blocks now,
And we'll haul aloft, now.
That'll be enough, now.

SONGS OF ROVING AND RAKING

The songs in this and the ensuing sections are largely of American origin. Those that are not have gone through quite a bit of Americanization—call it good or call it bad, America has put its stamp on these songs, and it is unmistakable. They have neither the tolerant acceptance of the ways of a man and a maid that the Scots songs have, nor do they have any high-flown metaphor or literary pretentions that mark the Elizabethan songs. They usually have three characteristics: wild exaggeration in the Paul Bunyan vein, as in the "Big Wheel," startling images, such as in "The Lehigh Valley," and a profusion of dirty words, exemplified by "Lulu." Gone is the pretense of subtlety (for it was always pretense—the Elizabethan songs as a whole are no more subtle than "The Big Wheel" and are considerably less so than "The Pioneers," a song practically without a printable word in it). In its place is an attempt to be heroically obvious. Matters are stated, then exaggerated. Whereas the Englishman or Scotsman finds it sufficient to describe a seduction, the American demands a twist or a punch line. The Elizabethan song, "The Jolly Tinker," describes the willing seduction of a woman by a travelling tinker, and is content with that. Its American counterpart gleefully makes the tinker rupture her vagina as well, and then go on to practice his wiles on all the devils of Hell. Some of these songs are clever, some, like "Lulu," are so straightforwardly crude that all one can do is laugh.

Zuleika

In spite of the Persian setting, this song has no Eastern origins, other than, perhaps, Boston. The Eastern motif is not at all unusual in folksong—"Kafoozalum," for example, is another one. All indications are that this is of fairly recent origin. (*3, 11, 17-II*)

The Jolly Tinker

This is a late descendant of another song by the same name (see Elizabethan Songs). The song has become Americanized through the years with the addition of some wilder verses. The editors have heard this song sung with no reference to Hell, and also with verses describing the tinker's frolic in Hades with no woman mentioned. It seems possible that this song is really a joining of two separate ballads, one about the adventures of a rake in Hell, and another which is closer to the Elizabethan version. (*1, 3, 11, 17-III*)

Little Ball of Yarn

An old and well-known story, this particular telling probably dates back to the time of Shakespeare. The last verse (probably a recent addition anyway) is usually bowdlerized in a fashion which leaves it no less suggestive than it was in its original version. We have included both forms as a lesson in style for the up-and-coming young censor. (*3, 11, 17-II*)

Poor Lil

The references to hashish, pernicious anemia, and the fractured French thrown in make it seem unlikely that this song has been circulating orally for any length of time. Oscar Brand puts its age at at least twenty-five years and refuses to divulge more. Be it as it may, it's a good song and one doesn't have to be French to understand it. (*1, 11, 17-I*)

Lil, Poor Lil

Again we have a song on the demise of a *fille-de-joie*, Lil, who must have died a thousand different musical deaths by now. This also sings well to the tune of "Poor Lil," but the editors have heard it sung, appropriately enough, to "The Cockfight." (*1*)

The Gruen Watch Song

The tune is even more recent than the song, being added by one of the editors, who wanted to sing it. The text itself is quite recent and definitely from the West Coast. Madman Muntz, mentioned in the last verse, is a used-car salesman *cum* TV manufacturer of the post-WW II era in L. A. (*3*)

Humoresque

The melody is a classical piece by Dvorak, well known to all aspiring violinists and their neighbors. As might be expected, the text has absolutely no connection with the melody. The central theme of the song is summed up very neatly in one version:

> Station master's awfully fussy,
> Says it makes the station mussy,
> So if you must go, please use a sack.   (*3, 11, 17-III*)

The Bastard King of England

At one time or another this has been ascribed to almost every major writer of the late 19th century: Tennyson, Whitman, Dickens and even Whistler have been mentioned, but the most interesting (true or untrue) rumor is that it was the authorship of this song that prevented the knighting of Rudyard Kipling by the (legitimate) Queen of England. During WW I, the song was considered to be invariably good for a fight "from any of the more imperialistic of the near-by Limeys." Pay close attention, for the plot twists and turns like a cat caught in a ball of yarn. (*1, 17-III*)

Seven Old Ladies

To the tune of "Oh, Dear, What Can the Matter Be," this rather sophisticated parody is another song which can be (almost) safely sung in mixed company. Since the verses can be sung in any order the singer pleases, most singers have a bit of trouble in getting all seven ladies safely inside, but this is all right since most audiences have probably lost count by this time, too. (*17-III*)

Bella

Beneath this haunting melody and simple story there lies a moral. Heed it well, all ye fair and tender maidens. (*17-III*)

Redwing

This is a rollicking parody on a sentimental tear-jerker of the early 1900's. This parody evidently started almost simultaneously with the original song, and has been one of the most widely circulated bawdy songs ever since. The tune is a square dance favorite. Woody Guthrie wrote a union song, "The Union Maid," which starts:

> There once was a union maid
> Who never was afraid
> Of goons and ginks and company finks . . .

In the editors' opinion, our version is by far the best of the lot. (*1, 3, 17-III*)

No Balls at All

For some unexplained reason Oscar Brand sings it under the title, "No Hips at All." We suppose that Pete Seeger would sing it as "No Dough at All" and further research will probably reveal that Joe Hill wrote a parody for the Wobblies called "No Boss at All." This is the way we hear it. (*3, 11*)

Tom Bolynn

Sometimes known as "Tumble Lynn," it is of the same general family of songs as "Duncan Macleerie." Its protagonist is the same poor but well-meaning simpleton who solves each of life's many problems in his characteristically muddled way. The song can be anything from the gentlest social satire to the most gruesomely ribald song extant; the verses here stand somewhere in the middle of the spectrum. (*1, 17-IV*)

The Big Bamboo   (*16, 26*)

Next Thanksgiving

What can one say about a song like this? (*3*)

My God, How the Money Rolls In

"My Bonnie Lies Over the Ocean" seems to pick up different sets of words, all somewhat less serious than the original. The editor can remember one learned in the sixth grade:

> My Bonnie lies over the ocean,
> My Bonnie lies over the sea,
> My father lies over my mother
> And that is how they got me.   (*3, 11, 17-IV*)

My Mother Chose My Husband

This song, with its Elizabethan lilt, pokes fun at virgin marriage, without ever resorting to specifics. This version is probably recent in origin, and was learned from the singing of Andrew Roland Summers on an early Folkways recording. (*25*)

Do Your Balls Hang Low?

The tune to this is "Continental Soldiers," a favorite with the nursery school set. The parody is quite widespread. (*1, 3*)

The Professions Song

The words to this song are a play on the double meanings of many common words, and is the only musical shaggy dog story we know. We wrote this song to sing at *librarians'* and *education* parties, in order to clear the air, without seeming to be "offensive." The verses about the electrician, politician and gynecologist can best be left to your imagination.

The Bonny Brown Hare

This song is very similar to the Elizabethan songs. It is completely dependent upon the pun on "hare," and the whole song is made up of this type of double meaning with only a single interpretation. (*2*)

Old Maclelland

The story itself is fairly common, but here it is distinguished by some colorful cowboy lingo. Few authors have managed to describe anything more completely and compactly than, "He then uncoiled his lariat and opened his hondo." (*2*)

ZULEIKA

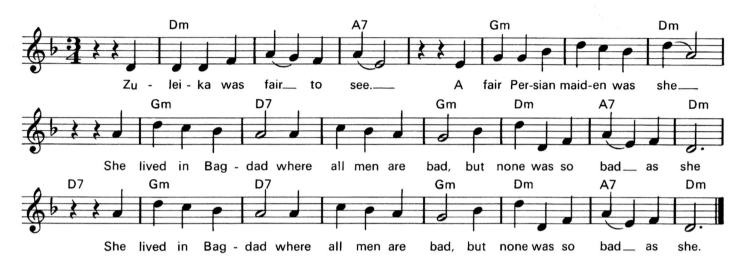

Zu - lei - ka was fair to see. A fair Per-sian maid-en was she

She lived in Bag - dad where all men are bad, but none was so bad as she

She lived in Bag - dad where all men are bad, but none was so bad as she.

Zuleika was fair to see,
A fair Persian maiden was she,
She lived in Baghdad, where all men are bad,
But none were so bad as she,
Yes she lived in Baghdad, where all men are bad,
But none were as bad as she.

Her husband was very old,
With millions in silver and gold,
He kept her locked in, away from all sin,
For Persians are very bold.

On her head she wore a turban
Which came from the looms of Iran,
Where no one could see she kept a small key,
Which she threw out again and again.

The first time she threw the key out,
It fell by the old water spout.
She sighed and she cried and the door opened wide,
And in walked her lover, Mahout.

The next time she threw out the key,
It fell by the old banyan tree.
She sighed and she cried and the door opened wide,
And in walked her lover, Ali.

She threw out the key once again,
Expecting her lover Suleiman.
She sighed and she cried and the door opened wide,
And in walked a whole caravan.

The leader then bowed his head low,
Expecting her wishes to know.
"The most of you stay," Zuleika did say,
But the children and camels must go.

New words & New music adaptation by Oscar Brand.
TRO—©Copyright 1970 Hollis Music, Inc., New York, New York.
Used by permission.

THE JOLLY TINKER

There was a jol-ly tink-er and he came from France. There was a jol-ly tink-er and he came from France, he came o-ver just to fid-dle, fuck and dance, with his long John fid-dle, whack-er, o-vergrown kid-ney crack-er, look-ing for a scrim-mage be-low the bel-ly band.

There was a jolly tinker, and he came from France. (2)
He came over just to fiddle, fuck, and dance.
   With his long John diddly wacker, over-grown kidney cracker,
   Looking for a scrimmage below the belly band.

One night the Queen was coming from the Royal Christmas Ball, (2)
And she saw the jolly tinker leaning up against the wall.

Said the tinker to the Queen, "Have you any little crack?" (2)
"Have you any little crack for a tinker to attack?"

Said the Queen to the tinker, "Yes, I have a little crack," (2)
"Yes, I have a little crack that a tinker might attack."

Oh he had her on the sofa and he had her on a chair, (2)
If he'd had a pair of wings, he'd have had her in the air.

He had her in the parlor and he had her in the hall. (2)
"My God," cried the chambermaid, "he's going to have us all."

"My God," cried the Queen, "I thought that I was able, (2)
But he split my vagina from my asshole to my navel."

Oh, the tinker, he died and he went to Hell, (2)
But he fucked all the devils and he fucked them very well.

New words & music by Oscar Brand.
©Copyright 1951, 1960 Oscar Brand, New York. Used by permission.

LITTLE BALL OF YARN

In the mer-ry month of June when the ros-es were in bloom, the birds were sing-ing gai-ly on the farm. When I spied a pret-ty miss and po-lite-ly asked her this, will you let me spin your lit-tle ball of yarn. Ball of yarn, Ball of yarn, It was then I spun her lit-tle ball of yarn. Ball of yarn.

In the merry month of June, when the roses were in bloom,
The birds were singing gaily on the farm;
When I spied a pretty miss and politely asked her this:
"Will you let me spin your little ball of yarn?
    Ball of yarn, ball of yarn,
    Will you let me spin your little ball of yarn?
    Ball of yarn, ball of yarn,
It was then I spun her little ball of yarn.

Well then she gave her consent and behind the fence we went;
I promised her that I would do no harm.
Then I gently laid her down and I ruffled up her gown;
It was then I spun her little ball of yarn.

It was nine months after that, in a pool room where I sat,
Never thinking I had done her any harm.
When a gentleman in blue said, "Young man we're after you,
You're the father of a little ball of yarn."

So in my prison cell I sit with my fingers dipped in shit
And the shadow of my cock upon the walls;
And the women as they pass thrust their hatpins up my ass
And the little birds play billiards with my balls.

*Note: That is the way the last verse goes; if you prefer to
bowdlerize it, this is the approved method (as expounded by
Oscar Brand in his book,* Bawdy Songs and Backroom Ballads.)

In the prison cell I sit, with my bathrobe in the shade,
And the shadow of my nose up the walls,
And the women as they pass thrust their hatpins up my coat,
And the little mice play hopscotch with my shoes.

New words & New music adaptation by Oscar Brand. ©Copyright 1951, 1960
Oscar Brand, New York. Used by permission.

Poor Lil

Her name was Lil and she was a beau-ty, she lived in a house of ill re-pu-ty
Gen-tle-men came from miles to see Lil-lian in her des - ha - bille.

Version A

Her name was Lil and she was a beauty,
She came from a house of III Reputy,
Gentlemen came from miles to see
Lillian in her deshabille.

She was comely, she was fair,
She had lovely golden hair,
But she drank too deep of the demon rum,
She smoked hashish and opium.

Day by day her form grew thinner
From insufficient protein in her.
She grew two hollows in her chest,
Why she had to go around completely dressed.

Now clothes may make a gal go far
But they have no place on a fille de joie,
Lillian's troubles started when
She concealed her abdomen.

She took to treatments in the sun,
She drank of Scotts Emul-si-on,
Three times daily she took yeast,
But still her clientele decreased.

For you must know her clientel-le
Rested chiefly on her belly,
She rolled that thing like the deep Pacific
It was something calorific.

She went to the house physician
To prescribe for her condition,
"You have got," the doc did say,
"Pernicious anem-i-a."

As Lillian lay in her dishonor,
She felt the hand of the Lord upon her,
She said, "My sins I now repents,
But, Lord, that'll cost you fifty cents."

LIL, POOR LIL

Version B

She was the best our camp produced
And them that ain't been screwed by Lil
Ain't had no goose and never will,
For Lil's been took away.

'Twas a standing bet around our town,
That no one could screw her and clamp her down
For when she screwed, she screwed for keeps,
And piled her victims up in heaps.

But down from the north came Yukon Pete,
With sixteen pounds of rolling meat.
When he laid his cock out on the bar,
The damn thing reached from here to thar.

We all knew Lil had met her fate
But we couldn't back down that thar late,
So it was arranged down by the mill,
Back of the schoolhouse on the hill.

When all the boys could get a seat
And watch that half-breed bury his meat,
Lil started out like the autumn breeze
Whistling through the hemlock trees.

She tried the twist and the double bunt
And all the tricks what's known to cunt,
But Pete was with her every lick
And just kept reeling out more prick.

At last poor Lil just had to stop,
For Pete had nailed her to the spot.
Her clothes were torn and ripped to shreds,
And scattered all over the cactus beds.

The sod was ripped for miles around
Where poor Lil's ass had hit the ground
But she died game I'm here to tell,
Died with her boots on where she fell—
So what the hell boys, what the hell!

THE GRUEN WATCH SONG

Shirley was a burley-cutie, dancing in the line.
She smiled out at the front row, and I knew that she was mine,
I asked to take her home and she was sweet as she could be.
The next day was her birthday and she wanted jewelry.
    So I gave her a gorgeous Gruen
    And the movement drive her mad
    Then she murmured as we kissed,
    "Gee it's curved to fit the wrist,"
    It was the best time piece she ever had.

Now Helen, she was sellin' down at Woolworth number nine,
She smiled across the counter and I knew that she was mine.
That mean old store detective, he was mad as he could be,
For what she sold to other guys she gave to me for free.

Now Lucy played Debussy on a clarinet so fine.
She smiled across the footlights and I knew that she was mine.
She played for me one night and I was certainly impressed—
Her lips did half the work and boy, her fingers did the rest.

Now Mabel waited table up at Hollywood and Vine,
She smiled at me so pretty that I thought that she was mine.
She asked me for a Cadillac and I felt like a dunce,
Playing second fiddle to a jerk like Madman Muntz.

Humoresque

Pass - en - gers will please re - frain from flush - ing toi - lets while the train is
stand - ing in the sta - tion I love you. We en - cour - age con - sti - pa - tion
while the train is in the sta - tion, moon - light al - ways makes me think of you.

Passengers will please refrain from flushing toilets while the train
Is standing in the station, I love you,
We encourage constipation while the train is in the station,
Moonlight always makes me think of you.

If you wish to pass some water, kindly try the pullman porter,
He'll place a vessel in the vestibule,
If the porter isn't here then try the platform in the rear,
The one in front is likely to be cool.

If the woman's room be taken, never feel the least forsaken,
Never show a sign of sad defeat,
Try the men's room cross the hall, and if some man has had the call,
He'll courteously relinquish you his seat.

If these efforts all are vain, then simply break the window pane,
This novel method used by very few,
We go strolling thru the park, goosing statues in the dark,
If Sherman's horse can take it, why can't you?

New words & New music adaptation by Oscar Brand.

THE BASTARD KING OF ENGLAND

MUSIC A

Now the min-strels sing of an Eng-lish King, man-y long years a-go, He ruled his land with an i-ron hand tho' his mo-rals were weak and low. His on-ly out-er gar-ment was a dir-ty yel-ler shirt with which he tried to hide his hide but he could-n't hide the dirt, he was dir-ty and lous-y and full of fleas and his ter-ri-ble tool hung down to his knees, God bless the Bas-tard King of Eng - land.

MUSIC B

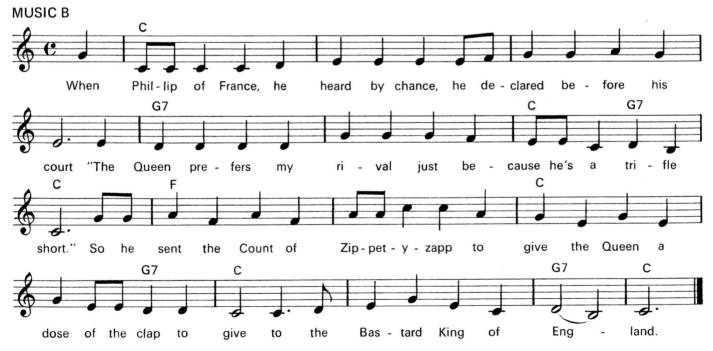

When Phil-lip of France, he heard by chance, he de-clared be-fore his court "The Queen pre-fers my ri-val just be-cause he's a tri-fle short." So he sent the Count of Zip-pet-y-zapp to give the Queen a dose of the clap to give to the Bas-tard King of Eng - land.

New words & music by Oscar Brand. ©Copyright 1953 Oscar Brand, New York. Used by permission.

MUSIC A

Now the minstrels sing of an English King, many long years ago,
He ruled the land with an iron hand though his morals were weak and low.
His only outer garment was a dirty yellow shirt
With which he tried to hide his pride, but couldn't hide the dirt.
  He was dirty and lousey and full of fleas
  And his terrible tool hung down to his knees;
  God Bless the Bastard King of England.

MUSIC A

The Queen of Spain was an amourous Jane, a sprightly wench was she,
She loved to fool with the royal tool of the king across the sea.
So she sent a royal message with a royal messenger
To invite the King of England to spend the night with her.
  He was dirty and lousey and full of fleas
  And his terrible tool hung down to his knees;
  God Bless the Bastard King of England.

MUSIC B

When Phillip of France, he heard by chance, he declared before his court
"The Queen prefers my rival just because I'm a triffle short"
So he sent the Count of Zippety Zapp to give the Queen a dose of the clap
To give to the Bastard King of England.

MUSIC A

When the King of England heard the news outside the castle walls
He up and swore by the royal whore, he'd have that Frenchman's balls.
So he offered half the royal purse and a piece of Queen Hortence
To any British subject who would nut the King of France.
  For he was dirty and lousey and full of fleas
  And his terrible tool hung down to his knees;
  God Bless the Bastard King of England.

MUSIC B

The Earl of Sussex jumped on his horse and straightway rode to France
He swore he was a Fairy so the King took down his pants
Then he slipped a thong around the prong, jumped on his horse and galloped along
Dragging the Frenchman back to England.

MUSIC A

When the King of England saw the sight he fainted on the floor,
For during the ride his rival's pride had stretched a yard or more.
Then all the maids in England came down to London Town,
And shouted round the battlements, "To Hell with the British Crown!"
  So Phillip of France usurped the throne,
  His sceptre was the royal bone
  With which he bitched the Bastard King of England.

SEVEN OLD LADIES

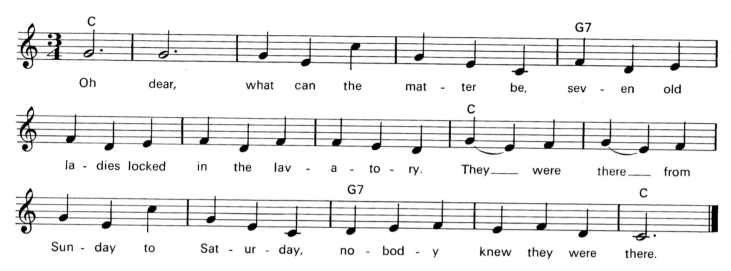

Oh   dear,   what can   the   mat - ter   be,   sev - en   old

la - dies locked   in   the   lav - a - to - ry.   They___ were   there___ from

Sun - day   to   Sat - ur - day,   no - bod - y   knew   they   were   there.

Oh, dear, what can the matter be
Seven old ladies locked in the lavatory
They were there from Sunday to Saturday
Nobody knew they were there.

The first was an athletic lady named Myrtle
Who vaulted the top like a steeple-chase hurdle
But her glasses got caught in the stay of her girdle
And nobody knew she was there.

The next was a lady named Jennifer Pymm
Who only sat down on a personal shim
But somehow got pinched twixt the cup and the brim
And nobody knew she was there.

The third was a lady, Elizabeth Bender
Who was doing all right till a vagrant suspender
Got all tangled up in her feminine gender
Nobody knew she was there.

The fourth was a lady named Abigail Humphry
Who settled right down just to make herself comfy
But then she found she could not get her bum free
Nobody knew she was there.

The next was a lady, Elizabeth Bickle
Who got herself into a terrible pickle
She stopped in a paybooth and hadn't a nickel
Nobody knew she was there.

The sixth was a woman called Emily Stover
And though she was known as a bit of a rover
She liked it so much that she thought she'd stay over
Nobody knew she was there.

The last was the Bishop of Chichester's daughter
Who went in to pass some superfluous water
She pulled on the chain and the rising tide caught her
Nobody knew she was there.

Bella

Softly

Bel-la was young__ and Bel-la was fair, with soft blue eyes__ and gold-en hair. O un-hap-py Bel-la. Her voice was light and her step was gay but she had no sense__ and one fine day. She got her-self put in a fam-il-y way by a mean and wick-ed, heart-less cru-el de-cei-ver.__

Bella was young and Bella was fair
With soft blue eyes and golden hair,
Oh, unhappy Bella.
Her voice was light and her step was gay,
But she had no sense so one fine day,
She got herself put in a family way
By a mean and wicked
Heartless, cruel deceiver.

She went to his flat but the dirty skunk
Had packed his bag and done a bunk,
Oh, unhappy Bella.
Her landlady said, "Get out, you whore!"
"Don't cross my threshold or darken my door."
Bella was put to affliction sore
By a mean and wicked,
Heartless, cruel deceiver.

Bella walked out through the ice and snow
What she went through, nobody will know,
Oh, unhappy Bella.
When the morning dawned so red,
Alas, alas, poor Bella was dead,
Sent in her youth to a lonely bed
By a mean and wicked,
Heartless, cruel deceiver.

So we see, do what we will,
The fruits of sin are suffering still,
Oh, unhappy Bella.
As Bella was put in her grave so low,
The men said, "Alas, but life it is so,"
But the women were chanting sweet and low,
"It's all the men, they've done it again, the bastards."

New words & music by Oscar Brand. ©Copyright 1950 Oscar Brand, New York. Used by permission.

REDWING

There once was an Indian maid, Who always was a-fraid, That some buck-a-roo would fly a-round her flue, As she lay sleep-ing in the shade. She had an i-dea grand, she'd fill it up with sand To keep the boys from hid-den joys and Red-wing's prom-ised land. Oh, the moon shines down on pret-ty Red-wing As she lay sleep-ing, This buck came creep-ing _____ With his one good eye he was a peep-ing. He hoped to reach the prom-ised land.

There once was an Indian maid, who always was
 afraid
That some buckaroo would fly around her flue
While she lay sleepin' in the shade.
She had an idea grand, she'd fill it up with sand,
To keep the boys from her hidden joys
And Redwing's promised land.
 Oh, the moon shines down on pretty Redwing,
 As she lay sleeping, this buck come creeping,
 With his one good eye he was a peeping,
 He hoped to reach the promised land.

Now he was an Indian wise, he reached for Redwing's
 thighs.
With an old rubber boot on the end of his toot
He made poor Redwing open up her eyes.
But when she came to life, she grabbed her Bowie
 knife,
It flashed in the sky as she let it fly,
And shortened his love life.
 Oh, the sun shines down on pretty Redwing,
 As she lies snoring there hangs a warning,
 A pair of Indian rocks adorning
 The flap of her wigwam door.

Oh girls if you want to be wives, put away those
    knives,
Boys like to play for a fling in the hay,
They don't want to pay the rest of their lives.
Mind what mama said, if you're lying in your bed,
"If you can't obey, don't reach for a blade,
Have a hell of a time instead."
    Oh, the clouds go floatin' over Redwing,
    As she lay snoring, her life was boring,
    Why she'd even welcome Hermann Goering
    Into the pleasure of her promised land.

NO BALLS AT ALL

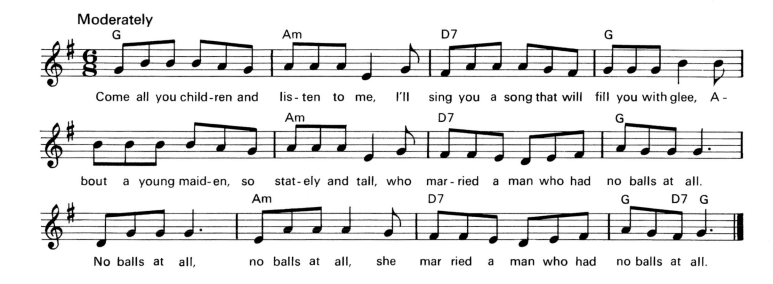

Moderately

Come all you child-ren and lis-ten to me, I'll sing you a song that will fill you with glee, A-
bout a young maid-en, so stat-ely and tall, who mar-ried a man who had no balls at all.
No balls at all, no balls at all, she mar ried a man who had no balls at all.

Come all you young children, and listen to me
I'll sing you a song that will fill you with glee.
About a young maiden, so stately and tall
Who married a man who had no balls at all.
    No balls at all, no balls at all,
    She married a man who had no balls at all.

The night of the wedding she crept into bed,
(Her cheeks were so rosy, her ass was so red);
She reached for his penis, his penis was small,
She reached for his balls, he had no balls at all.

"Mother, oh Mother, oh what shall I do?
I've married a man who's unable to screw."
"Oh daughter, oh daughter, don't feel so bad,
It's the very same trouble I had with your dad."

"Oh Mother, oh Mother, I wish I were dead,
There is no relief for my poor maidenhead."
"Oh daughter, the iceman will answer the call
Of the wife of the man who has no balls at all."

This daring young daughter took mother's advice
And laid with the man who delivers the ice;
A bouncing young baby was born in the fall
To the wife of the man who had no balls at all.

Tom Bolynn

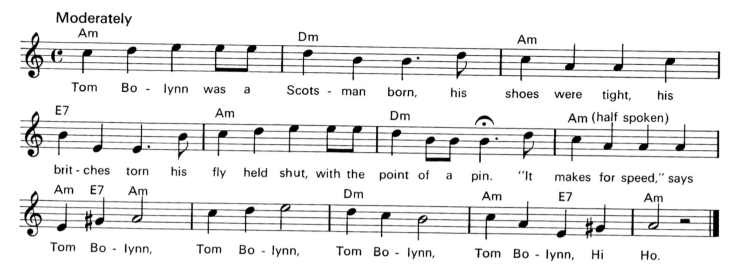

Moderately

Tom Bo-lynn was a Scots-man born, his shoes were tight, his
brit-ches torn his fly held shut, with the point of a pin. "It makes for speed," says
Tom Bo-lynn, Tom Bo-lynn, Tom Bo-lynn, Tom Bo-lynn, Hi Ho.

Tom Bolynn was a Scotsman born,
His shoes were tight, his britches torn,
His fly held shut with the point of a pin,
"It makes for speed," says Tom Bolynn.
Tom Bolynn, Tom Bolynn, Tom Bolynn, Hi Ho.

Tom Bolynn went courtin' one night,
The girl and her mother stripped for a fight.
They scratched and they bit in their naked skin,
"I'll marry you both," said Tom Bolynn.

Now, Tom Bolynn had an old grey mare,
She served as a wife for many a year,
But she got too old and he had to give in,
"She'll do for courting," said Tom Bolynn.

Now Tom came home from his journey's end,
He found his wife in bed with a friend.
The night was cold and the blankets thin,
"I'll sleep in the middle," said Tom Bolynn.

Now Tom Bolynn had a mangy cur
With ratty tail and ragged fur.
He lay like dead till a bitch come in,
" 'Tis Lazarus risen," said Tom Bolynn.

He went to church just once in his life
Where they preached against laying with another
   man's wife.
They called it a shame and they called it a sin,
"But it keeps them happy," said Tom Bolynn.

Now, Tom Bolynn, he needed a coat,
So he borrowed the skin from a neighboring goat,
The horns at the middle he set with a grin,
"Wish they were mine," said Tom Bolynn.

But the goat skin itched till his skin was sore
So Tom, he vowed he'd wear it no more,
The skinny side out and the wooly side in,
"It tickles my balls," said Tom Bolynn.

New words & New music adaptation by Oscar Brand. TRO—©Copyright 1970 Hollis Music, Inc. New York, New York. Used by permission.

THE BIG BAMBOO

Tune: "Little Brown Jug"

I asked my woman, what should I do,
To make her happy and keep her true?
"There's only one thing I want from you,
A little piece of the Big Bamboo."

CHORUS:
For the Big Bamboo grows good and long,
The Big Bamboo grows straight and strong,
The Big Bamboo grows straight and tall,
And it pleases one and all.

I gave my woman a banana plant,
She said, "This sure looks elegant,
It's much too nice to go to waste
But it's much too soft to suit my taste."

I gave my woman a coconut,
She said, "Sir, this is okay, *but*
I know you want to be good to me,
What good's the nut without the tree?"

I gave my woman a sugar cane,
"Sweets for the sweet," I did exclaim,
She handed it back to my surprise,
She liked the flavor but not the size.

Ever since God created man
He's pleased his woman as best he can,
But I find women are always true
To the man who gives them the Big Bamboo.

NEXT THANKSGIVING

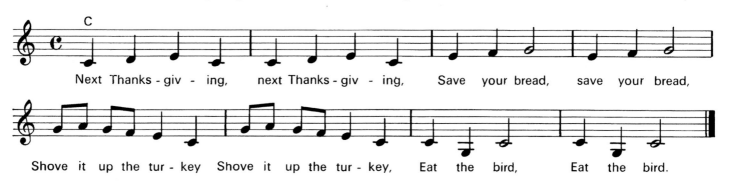

Next Thanksgiving, next Thanksgiving,
Save your bread, save your bread,
Shove it up the turkey, shove it up the turkey,
Eat the bird, eat the bird.

Next Christmas, next Christmas,
Save your tree, save your tree,
Shove it up the chimney, shove it up the chimney,
Goose St. Nick, goose St. Nick.

Next Easter, next Easter,
Save your eggs, save your eggs,
Shove 'em up the bunny, shove 'em up the bunny,
Eat the hare, eat the hare.

My God, How The Money Rolls In

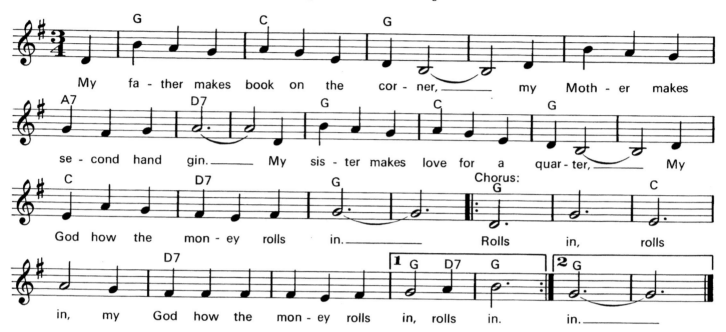

My father makes book on the corner,
My mother makes second hand gin,
My sister makes love for a quarter,
My God, how the money rolls in.

CHORUS:
Rolls in, rolls in,
My God, how the money rolls in, rolls in,
Rolls in, rolls in,
My God, how the money rolls in.

My brother's a poor missionary,
He saves fallen women from sin,
He'll save you a blonde for a dollar,
My God, how the money rolls in.

My uncle's an artist and painter;
He turns out a beautiful fin,
He sells them ten cents on the dollar,
My God, how the money rolls in.

My aunt is a boarding-house keeper,
She takes little working girls in;
They put a red light in the window,
My God, how the money rolls in.

My grandma sells cheap prophylactics,
She punctures the head with a pin,
For grandpa gets rich from abortions,
My God, how the money rolls in.

MY MOTHER CHOSE MY HUSBAND

My mother chose my husband and a lawyer's son was he,
When on our wedding night, he came to bed with me.
Ah, ha, ha, that's no way to, ah, ha, ha, that can't be.

When on our wedding night he came to bed with me,
He bit me on the shoulder and almost broke my knee.
Ah, ha, ha, that's no way to, ah, ha, ha, that can't be.

He bit me on the shoulder and almost broke my knee,
I called my waiting woman, "Come quickly Marjorie."
Ah, ha, ha, that's no way to, ah, ha, ha, that can't be.

Similarly

I called my waiting woman, "Come quickly Marjorie.
Go tell mamma I'm dying, bid her come hastily.

"Go tell mamma I'm dying, bid her come hastily."
Came momma to my bedside, before I could count three.

Came momma to my bedside, before I could count three.
"Cheer up my dear what ails you, will never kill," said she.

"Cheer up my dear what ails you, will never kill," said she.
"If I had died of that, my daughter, God knows where you would be."

"If I had died of that, my daughter, God knows where you would be.
"So if you die my daughter, I'll grave you splendidly."

"So if you die my daughter, I'll grave you splendidly.
"And put upon your tombstone where all mankind can see."

"And put upon your tombstone where all mankind can see,
'The only girl that couldn't survive that malady.' "
Ah, ha, ha, that's no way to, ah, ha, ha, that can't be.

DO YOUR BALLS HANG LOW?

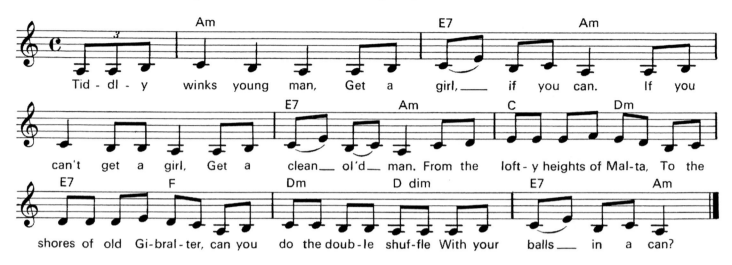

Tid - dl - y winks young man, Get a girl,___ if you can. If you
can't get a girl, Get a clean___ ol'd___ man. From the loft- y heights of Mal-ta, To the
shores of old Gi-bral-ter, can you do the doub-le shuf-fle With your balls___ in a can?

Tune: "Continental Soldiers"

Tiddlywinks, young man,
Get a girl if you can,
If you can't get a girl
Get a clean old man.

From the lofty heights of Malta
To the shores of old Gibraltar,
Can you do the double shuffle
With your balls in a can?

Do your balls hang low,
Do they wobble to and fro,
Can you tie them in a knot,
Can you tie them in a bow?

Do they make a rusty clamor
If you hit them with a hammer,
Can you do the double shuffle
If your balls hang low?

THE PROFESSIONS SONG

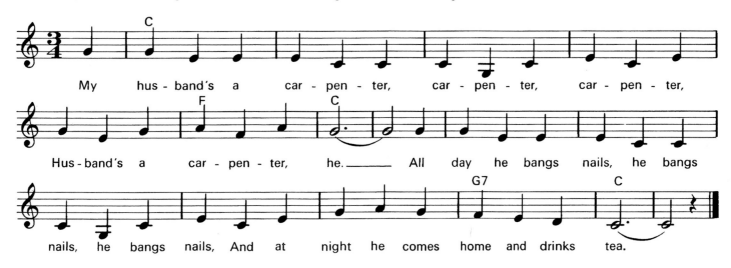

My hus-band's a car-pen-ter, car-pen-ter, car-pen-ter,

Hus-band's a car-pen-ter, he._____ All day he bangs nails, he bangs

nails, he bangs nails, And at night he comes home and drinks tea.

My husband's a carpenter, carpenter, carpenter,
Husband's a carpenter, he.
All day he bangs nails, he bangs nails, he bangs nails,
And at night he comes home and drinks tea.

My husband's a mason, a mason, a mason,
My husband's a mason, is he.
All day he lays bricks, he lays bricks, he lays bricks,
And at night he comes home and drinks tea.

My husband's a mechanic . . . .
All day he screws bolts . . . .

My husband's a farmer . . . .
All day he plows land . . . .

My husband's a postman . . . .
All day he licks stamps . . . .

My husband's a glassblower . . . .
All days he blows glass . . . .

My husband's a gourmet . . . .
All day he eats food . . . .

My husband's a husband, a husband, a husband,
My husband's a husband, is he
All day he drinks tea, he drinks tea, he drinks tea,
And at night he comes home and drinks coffee.

THE BONNY BROWN HARE

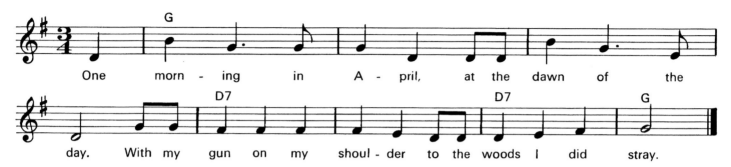

One morning in April, at the dawn of the day. With my gun on my shoulder to the woods I did stray.

One morning in April
At the dawn of the day,
With my gun on my shoulder
To the woods I did stray.

I met a fair maiden
Whose cheeks were of the rose
With her hair all down in ringlets
And her eyes black as coal.

I asked the fair maiden,
"Oh maiden so fair,
Could you tell me, o where, o where,
Could I find the brown hare?"

She answered me slowly,
She answered me low,
"Beneath my white petty,
The brown hare doth grow."

I laid her down gently
Beneath the shade of a tree,
And I cocked my big rifle,
Above her white knee.

She swooned and she fainted,
Her color all fled,
I stooped and I kissed her
For I thought she was dead.

Spoken:
Then she opened her eyes
Gently and said:

"Your aim is so true, sir,
Your bullets so fair—
Won't you fire once more
At my Bonny Brown Hare?"

"Oh, no, my fair maiden,
My powder is spent,
My bullets are gone and my ramrod is bent.
And I cannot fire on.

"But meet me tomorrow
'Neath the shade of a tree,
And if the weather proves fair,
I'll fire once more
At your Bonny Brown Hare."

Old Maclelland

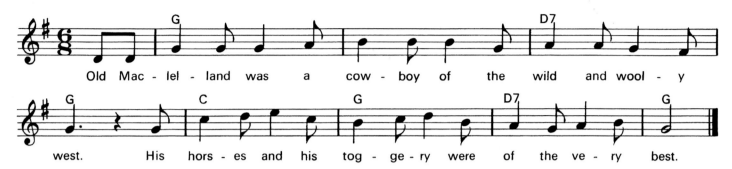

Old Mac - lel - land was a cow - boy of the wild and wool - y
west. His hors - es and his tog - ge - ry were of the ve - ry best.

Old Maclelland was a cowboy
Of the wild and wooly west.
His horses and his toggery
Were of the very best.

He had a pretty good education,
That is he was no fool,
The only fault Maclelland had,
He was handy with his tool.

Maclelland left that cow-camp;
'Twas on a Friday night,
He spied a pretty schoolmarm
In a schoolhouse painted white.

He sprang into the atmosphere
Stampeded dogs and cats,
And he hit the trail a-rolling
With the schoolmarm on the flats.

He reined his horse onto the gate.
He said, "May I come in?"
"You may," said the schoolmarm
With a kind of saucy grin.

He kicked the cowshit off his boots
And straightened his cravat,
And he entered through the doorway
With the schoolmarm on the flats.

He laid her on the bench—
The best that he could do;
He unwrapped his coil from off his horn
And opened his hondo.

Then bringing forth his roller
He stabbed her in the fat,
And stopped the wind from blowing
Through the schoolmarm on the flats.

He said, "I've diddled maids and maidens,
And Negro wenches and all that,
But the best I ever tackled
Was the schoolmarm on the flats.

But when he drained his roller,
Just nine days after that,
He found that he had shankers
From the schoolmarm on the flats.

Come all you jolly rounders,
And listen to my song;
Keep old John Henry in his chaps
And keep him fogging on.

And if he gets unruly,
Just fan him with your hat.
Remember old Maclelland
And the schoolmarm on the flats.

...For The Boys In The Back Room

The advance of mass media and literacy has caused a loss of many folksongs. However, the bawdy song remains almost unaffected by the commercial media. It has never been sung at polite gatherings, and can't be sung on radio or TV. The singer of bawdy songs doesn't have to compete with professionals. If he can croak the words understandably, he is a success. The proper habitat of these songs is the barracks, the stag party, and the drunken brawl. TV has made no inroads on these—if anything it has increased them by driving its watchers to drink. The bawdy song has been the one type of folk song to retain its popularity into the present age; it may soon be the sole survivor.

Little Piece of Wang

Learned in Springfield, Ohio, in 1961, this gentle explanation of sex manages to avoid any reference to the birds and the bees. Nevertheless, it is one of the most good-natured songs in the book.

The Hermit

A song well-suited to occasions where a dirty song would be inappropriate. (*11, 17-II*)

Anne Cooper Hewitt

Several decades ago there was a newspaper scandal when a mother was sued by her daughter, Anne Cooper Hewitt. Mrs. Hewitt had had her daughter sterilized. It was quite a sordid case: The reason for the sterilization had to do with a clause in Mr. Hewitt's will. The story remained in the headlines long enough for Gene Fowler to write this poem. (*1*)

Crusher Bailey

The real hero of this ballad was a Monmouth ironmaster, Cosher Bailey, who built the Taff Vale railway along the Aberdare Valley in 1846. He drove the first train over this railway himself, and according to legend, got stuck in the tunnel. The original song commemorated this achievement, but as time went on, people thought of other things which he might have done. The song was popular among Welsh-crewed sailing ships as a capstan shanty, sung to a tune from an older Welsh folk song, "Hoby Derry Don Do." Several of the verses of this version are evidently descended from the sea shanty, and the chorus still mixes the Welsh with the English words. "Sian fach fwyn"—sweet young Jane. Oscar Brand reports that the words, "hoby derry don do," are derived from a druidic incantation, and advises caution in their use. (*4, 11, 17-II*)

Perversity

Recently written in Illinois.

The Pioneers

If one can call any song charming which has so many unprintable words in it, it would certainly be this ironic report on the activities of our hardy pioneers. Dan'l Boone, Kit Carson, Paul Bunyan—those were mighty men and they don't make any more like them today—they sure as hell don't if this little song is accurate. It is at once a gigantic tall tale and a broad Rabelasian satire on the brave, noble heroes who founded our brave, noble nation every fourth of July. The tune, a variant of "Columbo," was added by the editors to conceal the embarrassing fact that they didn't know the real tune. (*1*)

Our Goodman

This version of the venerable ballad was originally published in *Count Vicarion's Book of Bawdy Ballads.* (*11, 16, 17-I*)

The Farmer and the Mockingbird

Recently written in Illinois.

The Virgin Sturgeon

The editors caution that while caviar is recommended, it is not guaranteed—the experimenting reader would do well to start with pocketbook-size portions, gradually increasing until the right dosage is discovered. *(1, 3)*

Sing a Song of Sixty-Nine

A college student has been defined as "one who can't count to seventy without laughing." Songs, jokes and remarks about the number sixty-nine outnumber all others, but we have limited ourselves to two of them in this volume. This one was probably written in Los Angeles about 1956. *(3, 16)*

The Sea Crab

"The Sea Crab," sometimes known as "The Crabfish," has the distinction of being the oldest known bawdy song which is still sung. It is known not only in the English-speaking world, but throughout Europe and even into Asia.

It unquestionably began life as a folk-tale rather than as a song. As such, it has been collected in such places as Finland, Bosnia, Italy, France, and even Indonesia. It probably started life as a European creation. The earliest mention of it is in the account of a traveler in Russia *ca* 1280. How it could get to Indonesia hasn't been established; one theory is that it came by way of India, though no Indian version has as yet been uncovered.

The folk-song version is relatively young, at least as far as is known. The first mention of it is in the *Percy Folio MS, 1620-1650*, so we know only that it has been in existence for at least three and a quarter centuries. The story has grown longer and more complicated. The folk-tale would end by having a passing traveler help the couple out of their strange predicament. The song, on the other hand, has added new complications, and shows signs of getting completely out of hand, just like "Columbo."

"The Sea Crab" has been collected in America fairly often, but there seems to be no single widespread version; almost every singer knows a completely different tune and chorus. This particular version was learned in Ohio and shows evidence of having spent a good part of its musical life in Ireland.

The bibliography on page 142 contains a reference to a more complete discussion of this song.

(12)

Dead-Eye Dick

This is known in fragmentary form to nearly every child past puberty. In order to get a singable version, it was necessary to re-write the six middle lines, which follow the original in the spirit if not the letter. Sing it to the tune of the "Ring Dang Doo." *(3, 11, 17-III)*

A Little Song

This wry comment on the tin-pan alley love ballad compresses all the usual sentiments into two verses with considerably more honesty than the juke-box does.

LITTLE PIECE OF WANG

When the good Lord made Father Adam, they say he laughed and sang,
Sewed him up the belly with a little piece of wang.
But when he'd got it finished, I guess he measured wrong,
For the piece he'd sewed him up with was very much too long.

"It's but eight inches long," said he, "I guess I'll let it hang,"
And he left on Adam's belly that little piece of wang,
But when he made Mother Eve, I bet it made him start,
For the piece he sewed her up with was very much too short.

"It leaves an awful crack," said he, "but I don't give a dang,
She can fight it out with Adam for that little piece of wang";
And ever since that ancient day when human life began,
There's been a constant wage of strife between a woman and a man,
For the woman swears to have that piece that on his belly hang,
To fill that awful crack that's left when the Lord ran out of wang.

So let us not be selfish, boys, with what the women lack,
But keep them busy on the wang to fill that crack,
For the good Lord never intended that it should idle hang
When he placed on Adam's belly that little piece of wang.

THE HERMIT

A her-mit there was— who lived in a dell— I'll swear to the truth of the sto ry I tell— for my grand-fa-ther's grand-fa-ther knew him quite well,— this her-mit who lived in the dell.———

A hermit there was who lived in a dell,
I'll swear to the truth of the story I tell,
For my grandfather's grandfather knew him quite
        well,
This hermit who lived in the dell.

He lived all alone by the side of the lake,
Concoctions and herbs for his food he would make,
And naught but a fish would the good man partake
On Friday.

Now, to ord'nary mortals his portals he closed,
Once a year he would bathe his body and clothes,
How the lake stood it the Lord only knows,
And he won't tell.

One morning he rose up all dripping and wet,
His horrified vision two ladies met,
Now in feminine matters he was no vet,
So he blushed.

He reached for his hat where it lay on the beach,
To cover up all that its wide brim would reach,
And then he cried out in a horrified screech,
"Go away."

But the maids only laughed at his piteous plight,
And begged him to show them the wonderful sight,
But he clutched at his hat and he held to it tight
To hide it.

Now just at that moment a wandering gnat
Made the hermit forget just where he was at,
He struck at the insect and let go the hat,
Oh, horrors.

And now I have come to the crux of my tale,
The hermit turned red and then he turned pale,
He offered a prayer, for prayers never fail,
So 'tis said.

Of the truth of the story there's no doubt at all,
The Lord heard his prayer and answered the call,
Though he let go the hat—yet, the hat didn't fall,
A blessed miracle!

ANNE COOPER HEWITT

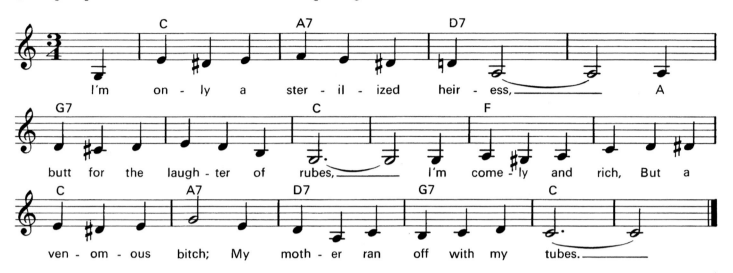

I'm on-ly a ster-il-ized heir-ess, _____ A
butt for the laugh-ter of rubes, _____ I'm come-ly and rich, But a
ven-om-ous bitch; My moth-er ran off with my tubes. _____

I'm only a sterilized heiress,
A butt for the laughter of rubes,
I'm comely and rich
But a venomous bitch—
My mother—ran off with my tubes.

Oh, fie on you, mother, you bastard,
Come back with my feminine toys,
Restore my abdomen,
And make me a woman,
I want to go out with the boys.

Imagine my stark consternation,
At feeling a surgeon's rude hands
Exploring my person,
(Page Aimee McPherson)
And then rudely snatching my glands.

Oh, fie on you, medical monsters,
How could you so handle my charms?
My bosom is sinking,
My clitoris shrinking—
I need a strong man in my arms.

The butler and second-man snub me,
No more will they use my door key;
The cook from Samoa
Has spermatozoa
For others, but never for me.

Oh, fie on you, fickle men servants!
With your strong predilection to whore,
Who cares for paternity,
Forgive my infirmity—
Can't a girl just be fun any more?

What ruling in court can repay me,
For losing my peas-in-the-pod?
My joyous fecundity,
Turned to morbundity,
Lilee Pickford, I'll have to try God.

Oh, fie on you, courthouse and ruling!
I want my twin bubbles of jest,
Take away my hot flashes
And menopause rashes,
And let me feel weight on my chest.

CRUSHER BAILEY

Wistfully

Crush - er Bail - ey went to col - lege, ho - bi der - ry don do, ____
For to get a lit-tle know-ledge, Sing it out a-gain, boys, ___ When the proc-ter saw him com-in',
Jane, sweet Jane, He went home to hide his wo-men, Jane, Jane come to the glen,
To sing praise of Sean foch foyn. Jane, Jane come to the glen, To sing praise of Sean foch foyn.

Crusher Bailey went to college,
Hoby deri dondo.
For to get a little knowledge,
Sing it out again, boys.
When the proctor saw him comin'
Jane, sweet Jane,
He went home to hide his woman,
Jane, Jane, come to the glen,
To sing praise of Sean Foch Foyn,
Jane, Jane, come to the glen,
To sing praise of Sean Foch Foyn.

Crusher Bailey went to college
For to pass matriculation.
But he saw a pretty barmaid
And he never left the station.

Crusher Bailey had a sister,
Laughed like blazes when you kissed her.
Couldn't knit nor darn no stocking,
But what she could do sure was shocking.

Crusher Bailey had a daughter,
All the men of town had sought her.
She worked all night and slept all day
And paused at times for a fling in the hay.

Listen while I sing a solo,
About his ship, the Marco Polo.
See her cutting thru the water,
I wish I were in bed with the captain's daughter.

Crusher Bailey had a stoker.
He thought himself a bloody joker.
Just to see the steam go higher,
He'd make water on the boiler.

Perversity

MUSIC A

Look at norm-al-i-ty think a-bout re-al-i-ty Pon-der con-ven-tion-al-i-ty Aren't they a fright-ful bore.___ Aren't they a fright-ful bore.___

MUSIC B

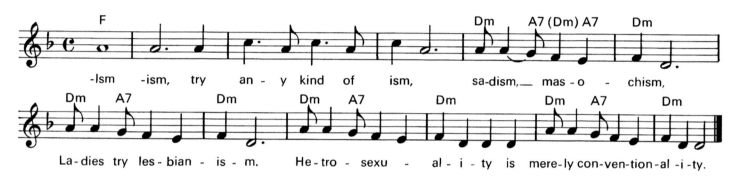

-Ism -ism, try an-y kind of ism, sa-dism,___ mas-o-chism, La-dies try les-bian-is-m. He-tro-sexu-al-i-ty is mere-ly con-ven-tion-al-i-ty.

MUSIC A

Look at normality
Think about reality
Ponder conventionality
Aren't they a frightful bore.

MUSIC A

I like perversity,
Something with diversity.
At this University
You'll find a trifle more. (2)

MUSIC B

Ism——Ism,
Try any type of ism.
Sadism, Masochism, ladies try Lesbianism.
Heterosexuality
Is merely Conventionality.

MUSIC B

Witch——Witch,
I'd like to be a witch.
If I were I'd put a hex
On every type of normal sex.
Fetishes take the place of this,
Nothing is better than a leather-bound disc.

MUSIC A

Pick your perversity,
Try Homosexuality.
Animals will never fail,
A horse, a cow or a puppy-dog's tail.
You'll only find Normality
In books about Sociology.

MUSIC A

Everybody is doing it,
And most of them aren't rueing it.
Try it once, I'm sure you'll say,
"I'll never have another boring day."
Normality is awfully bleak,
You will be warped by the end of the week.

THE PIONEERS

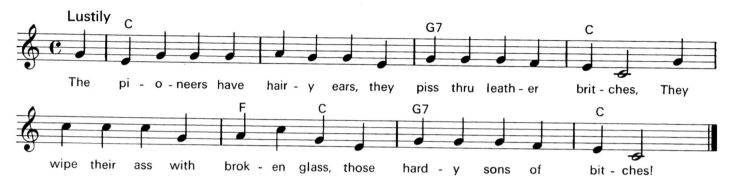

Lustily

The pi - o - neers have hair - y ears, they piss thru leath - er brit - ches, They wipe their ass with brok - en glass, those hard - y sons of bit - ches!

The pioneers have hairy ears,
They piss thru leather britches;
They wipe their ass on broken glass,
Those hardy sons-of-bitches!

When cunt is rare they fuck a bear,
(They knife him if he snitches.)
They knock their cock against the rocks,
Those hardy sons-of-bitches!

They take their ass upon the grass
From fairies or from witches;
Their two-pound dinks are full of kinks,
Those hardy sons-of-bitches!

Without remorse they fuck a horse
And beat him if he twitches;
Their mighty dicks are full of nicks,
Those hardy sons-of-bitches!

To make a mule stand for the tool
He's beat with hickory switches;
They use their pricks for walking sticks,
Those hardy sons-of-bitches!

Great joy they reap from bugg'ring sheep,
In sundry bogs and ditches,
Nor give a damn if he be a ram—
Those hardy sons-of-bitches!

When booze is rare, they do not care,
They take a shot of Fitch's,
They fuck their wives with butcher knives,
Those hardy sons-of-bitches!

OUR GOODMAN

When I got home on Saturday night as drunk as a cunt can be, I
saw a hat up-on the rack where
my old hat should be, so I said to my wife, the pride o' my life, "why aren't you true to
me?__ Whose hat is that up on the rack where my hat ought to be?" "O, you're
drunk you cunt, you sil-ly old cunt, you're drunk as a cunt, can be, that's not a hat, upon the rack but a cham-ber pot you see." In all the miles I've trav-eled,__ a
mil-lion miles or more, A cham-ber pot with a hat-band on I nev-er seen be-fore.

When I got home on Saturday night as drunk as a
   cunt can be,
I saw a hat upon the rack where my old hat
   should be,
So I said to the wife, the pride o' my life,
Why aren't you true to me? Whose hat is that
   upon the rack
Where my old hat should be?
      Oh you're drunk you cunt,
      You silly old cunt,
      You're as drunk as a cunt can be,
      That's not a hat upon the rack
      But a chamber pot you see.

In all the miles I've traveled, a million miles or
   more,
A chamberpot with a hatband on I never seen
   before.

(similarly:)
I saw a head upon the bed where my old head
   should be.
      "That's not a head upon the bed
      But a baby's bum you see."
A baby's bum with whiskers on I never did see
   before.

I saw a nob betwixt her legs where my old nob
   should be;
      "That's not a nob betwixt my legs
      But a rolling pin you see."
A rolling pin with balls attached I never have
   seen before.

I saw a mess on her nightdress where my old
   mess should be;
      "That's not a mess upon my dress
      But clotted cream you see."
Some clotted cream that smelt of fish I never
   have smelt before.

97

THE FARMER AND THE MOCKINGBIRD

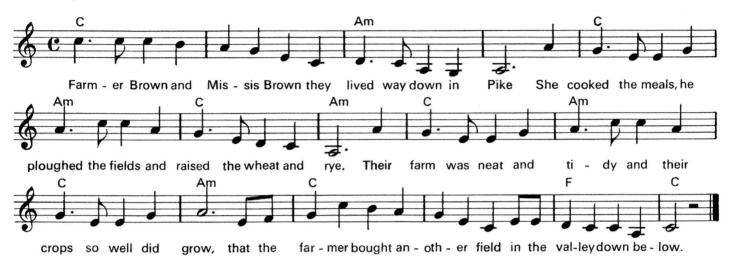

Farm - er Brown and Mis - sis Brown they lived way down in Pike She cooked the meals, he ploughed the fields and raised the wheat and rye. Their farm was neat and ti - dy and their crops so well did grow, that the far - mer bought an - oth - er field in the val-ley down be - low.

Farmer Brown and Mrs. Brown, they lived way
    down in Pike.
She cooked the meals, he plowed the fields and
    raised the wheat and rye.
Their farm was neat and tidy and their crops so
    well did grow
That the farmer bought another field in the valley
    down below.

This field was down the mountainside about a
    mile away
And Brown would rise at six o'clock and work all
    through the day.
He ploughed and pushed and pulled and sweat as
    'hind the plow he trod;
So tired was he when he got home that he could
    not raise a rod.

The farmer's wife to find this out was very much
    surprised.
She pulled and poked and rubbed and stroked
    but could not make it rise.
"My dear," said she, "I'm much afraid if you
    can't be a man,
That I'll have to find my loving just at any place
    I can."

So they thought the matter over and this idea
    they did heed:
That Farmer Brown would plow the fields until
    he felt the need.
And then would he give whistles three both very
    loud and clear,
And his wife would come a-running for to satisfy
    her dear.

So the farmer he would whistle and his wife
    would leave the house;
The mule would slowly pull the plow while the
    farmer plowed his spouse.
But there was a cunning mockingbird who nearby
    lived his life,
And soon found he that whistles three would
    always bring the wife.

He'd whistle every hour, and out the wife would
    fly,
Till she was so God damn tired that she could not
    bat an eye.
Then matters they got worse and worse and soon
    got out of hand
And the farmer he was forced to go and get a
    hired hand.

So now they all are happy and peace reigns on
the farm,
The new field is a-growing and much money it
does earn;
The farmer plows upon the field and walks
behind the hitch,
While the man he hired stays behind and rides
upon his bitch.

Now farmers, if you have two fields a-needing of
the plow
And can only work on one of them, well listen to
me now.
Just put yourself on one of them and do the best
you can;
And to plow and sow the other—why, just get a
hired man.

THE VIRGIN STURGEON

Cav - i - ar comes from a vir - gin stur-geon, Vir - gin sturgeon is a ve-ry good fish,

No good stur-geon, wants to be a vir - gin, That's why cav-iar's a ve - ry good dish.

Caviar comes from the virgin sturgeon
Virgin sturgeon is a very good fish.
No good sturgeon wants to be a virgin,
That's why caviar's a very rare dish.

I fed caviar to my girl friend,
She's my girl friend tried and true.
Now my girl friend needs no urgin',
I recommend caviar to you.

I fed caviar to my grandpa,
He was a man of ninety-three.
Screams and cries were heard from grandma,
Grandpa had her up a tree.

I put caviar in the soda,
That livened up the party, sure.
What am I doing stripped down naked?
Though these girls were sweet and pure.

I fed caviar to my mistress,
She always did it cheerfully.
Now she does it with a vengeance,
Oh, my God, it's killing me.

Little Mary went sleigh riding,
And the sled turned up-side-down.
Little Mary started singing,
Massa's in the cold, cold ground.

The policeman came to visit one day,
Postman came and went away.
The baby came just nine months later,
Who fired the shot, the blue or the grey?

SING A SONG OF SIXTY-NINE

Sing a love song, Sing a pae - an, Sing of plea - sures, yours and mine, but in all your hap - py vers - es, don't for - get old six - ty nine.

Tune: "Clementine"

Sing a love song, sing a paean,
Sing of pleasures, yours and mine,
But in all your happy verses
Don't forget old sixty-nine.

It's immoral, it's indecent,
It's repulsive—but sublime!
Though they tell me it's perversion,
Still I like to sixty-nine.

Hint it subtly, don't appall her,
She might feel it's less than fine;
Making love, but quite inversely,
She might not take to sixty-nine.

Sneak up on her, do not startle;
Let your kisses flow like wine.
But descend, ah, gently, gently,
As you sink to sixty-nine.

Let her fondle, let her feel it,
Virile tokens, one-third nine;
With your equipment then confront her,
She may rise to sixty-nine.

Kinsey tells us eggheads do it
More than peasants (those aren't fine);
Tell her it's a cultured pleasure;
She'll be hot for sixty-nine.

Once she learns how, once she tries it,
She may never stay supine!
('Tis a danger—one must face it)
She'll only want to sixty-nine.

Thus I tell you, see ye to it,
Lest your love get out of line.
Spice your wooing, but don't rue it,
Ration her on sixty-nine.

THE SEA CRAB

There was a lit-tle man and he had a lit-tle horse, sad-dle and a brid-le and he
threw his legs a-cross, sing-ing dad-dle dum, O mis-ter dad-dle dum day._____

He rode and he rode till he came to a brook.
There he spied a fisherman with a line and hook.

Fisherman, oh fisherman, will you tell this to me,
Have you got a crabfish you can give to me?

Oh yes, oh yes, I've one, two, three,
The biggest one I'll give to thee.

When he got home he couldn't find a dish,
So he threw it in the pot where the old lady pissed.

Well, his wife got up and she straddled the pot,
The dirty little crabfish grabbed her by the twat.

Oh husband, oh husband, as sure as I am born,
The devil's in the piss-pot and giving me the horn.

Then she gave a howl and a groan and a grunt,
And danced around the room with the crabfish on
     her cunt.

Old man jumped up, buttoned on his clothes,
Up jumped the crabfish and grabbed him by the nose.

Old woman, old woman, ain't this a pretty pass
To find my nose so close to your ass?

Old man, old man, well that's no crime,
For it's been there ten thousand times.

Old woman, old woman, can't you blow a little fart
To blow my nose and your ass apart?

Well, she heaved and she ho'd and she come a little bit,
And she filled the old man's face full of shit.

'Tis the end of my song and the moral it is this,
Always put your specs on before ye take a piss.

New words & music by Oscar Brand.
©Copyright 1953 Oscar Brand, New York. Used by permission.

DEAD-EYE DICK

Tune: "Ring Dang Doo" in Chapter 7.

Out of the woods came Dead-Eye Dick,
The man with a six-foot spiral prick;
He searched the earth in a mighty hunt
For a girl with a six-foot spiral cunt.

He searched by air and he searched by ground,
But never a six-foot twat he found.
He searched by land and he searched by sea,
But never a corkscrew screw screwed he.

He searched from Spain to the Isle of Wight,
To find a girl to fit him right;
At last, when he found her, he shot her dead—
For he found that she had a left-hand thread!

A LITTLE SONG

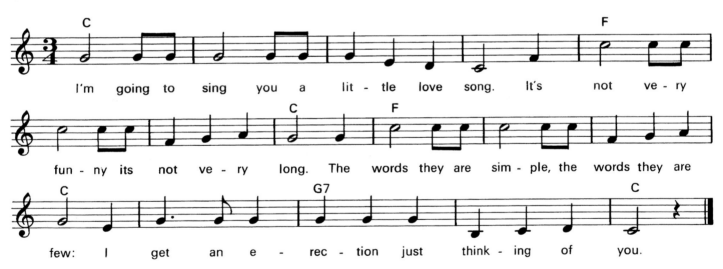

I'm going to sing you a lit - tle love song. It's not ve - ry fun - ny its not ve - ry long. The words they are sim - ple, the words they are few: I get an e - rec - tion just think - ing of you.

I'm going for to sing you a little love song,
It's not very funny, it's not very long.
The words they are simple, the words they are few:
I get an erection just thinking of you.

There's one more verse to this little song.
Just like the first one it's not very long.
The words they are simple, in fact rather plain:
My organs start throbbing at the sound of your name.

MARCHING SONGS OF OUR MIGHTY ARMIES

Your head shaved like the bald headed end of a broom, ninety days in the sun and muck, and on your feet from dawn to dusk. Then you get a three day pass and all you think of is broads. So the barracks have always been a hatchery for bawdy songs. The sweat of basic, the lilt of the cadence count and those long horney nights all combine in a rhythm of lust. Here are a few "chicks" that have cracked the shell.

I Don't Want to Join the Army

This was a popular song in the British army in both WW I and WW II. Make with a bit of a Cockney accent, Guv'nor, that's the chap! *(11)*

Roll Me Over

This was easily the best-known song in WW II. Some sang "Praise the Lord and Pass the Ammunition," some sang "Roger Young," but all sang "Roll Me Over." It is descended from a sea shanty used for pumping ship call, "Put Your Shoulder Next to Mine and Pump Away." See also "Shove It Home," page 00. *(3, 17-IV)*

Honey Babe

This song made the hit parade during the Korean War with a set of verses which were only slightly suggestive. The songwriter who put that version together probably had to go through quite a few verses to find any which would pass the radio censor. The "I've got a gal . . ." theme seems to lead to some wild fantasies—you should have seen the ones we didn't use.
(3, 16)

Do Your Balls Hang Low?

The song is so good we printed it twice. *(3)*

Hitler Has Only Got One Ball

The movie "Bridge on the River Kwai" opens with a scene showing a captured British platoon coming through the jungle whistling a tune usually known as the "Colonel Bogie March." The words, presented here, might explain why they were whistling instead of singing.

Roll Your Leg Over

This famous song has a tremendous pool of verses. The version in *SORAIR* was reportedly obtained when the guy who was putting it together went out in the hall and shouted, "Anybody know some verses to 'Roll Your Leg Over'?" Those not known were soon made up and he ended with three pages full of verses and would have had far more if he'd waited a few days longer. The tune, incidentally, is also known in Holland as "Louisa," a children's song.

An interesting note on one of the verses, which may give some insight into the mysterious way that dirty jokes come into existence: The phrase, "to plug in and grind," refers to the standard method of solving math or physics problems. Once one understands the problem and knows what formulas to apply, he can "plug in" these formulas and "grind out" the answer.

The Cal Tech student board of directors was discussing a beauty contest to be held in conjunction with the homecoming game. CIT being a men's institution, they had decided to go to a few neighboring colleges and recruit some candidates for the honor. As the discussion ended, one of the members stood up and said, quite seriously, "Well, that's that. All we have to do is plug in and grind." One or two parties later the verse, "I wish all young girls was solutions to find . . ." cropped up.

In the same way, dirty jokes probably originate in someone's chance remark which is repeated as an anecdote with more and more embellishments until it finally becomes a completed joke. *(3, 11, 17-I, 17-III)*

Barnacle Bill, the Sailor

This song has made quite a transformation since the days when it was a nursery song. There is at least one more Armed Forces version of this, called "Barnacle Bill the Pilot."

Way Up in Pennsylvania

The story is common among both martial and civilian folksongs, and the only reason for including it here rather than in another section is the pun in the last verse. The tune is "My Grandfather's Whiskers." (3)

Cats on the Rooftops

While this song might seem quite recent—some verses postdate neon lights—other verses barely postdate candles. Two extra verses are worth recording here, even though they didn't fit the song as printed.

> The Sergeant-Major has a hell of a life,
> He has no woman and he can't afford a wife,
> So he simply sticks it up the regimental fife
> And revels in the throes of fornication.

> The alligator, so it seems,
> Seldom ever has wet dreams,
> But when he comes he comes in streams
> As he revels in the throes of fornication. (1, 3, 11)

Bell Bottom Trousers

This was recently bowdlerized into a pop song. However, it goes back at least to early 19th century England and probably much earlier. An alternate third verse:

> I lifted up the blanket and a moment there did lie,
> He was on me, he was in me, in the twinkling of an eye,
> He was in again and out again and plowing up a storm,
> And the only word I thought to say, "I hope you're keeping warm." (1, 3, 11)

Mush, Mush, Mush, Touraliady

The tune and chorus are from a traditional Irish hooley song of the same name. The sentiments expressed are more modern, in point of time if not in point of view. The song was popular in the navy during the war, and has since matriculated to the colleges; it still rings through the hallowed halls of ivy on nights when a pint is likely to be found inside the most academic cap and gown. (3, 17-V)

I DON'T WANT TO JOIN THE ARMY

I don't want to be a soldier, don't want to be a man of Mars
I just want to go down to old So-ho pinch-ing all the gir-lies on the shoul-der blades. I don't need no for-eign wo-man,—— Lon-don's full of girls I nev-er had,—— I want to stay in Eng-land, Jol-ly, jol-ly, Eng-land, fol-low-ing in the foot-steps of my Dad. Gor-blim-ey call out the mem-bers of the Queen's Ma-rines, call out the Kings Ar-til-le-ry. Call out my moth-er,—— my sis-ter and my broth-er but for God's sake don't call me.

I don't want to be a soldier,
Don't want to be a man of Mars,
I just want to go down to old Soho,
Pinching all the girlies on the shoulder blades.
I don't need no foreign women,
London's full of girls I never had,
I want to stay in England, jolly, jolly England,
Following the footsteps of my Dad.

CHORUS:
Call out the members of the Queen's Marines,
Call out the King's Artillery,
Call out my mother, my sister, and my brother,
But for God's sake don't call me.

Monday night my hand was on her ankle,
Tuesday night my hand was on her knees,
Wednesday night, success, I lifted up her dress,
Thursday night I lifted up her silk chemise,
Friday night I got my hand upon it,
Saturday night I gave it just a tweak,
Sunday after supper, I finally got it up her,
And now I'm paying seven bob a week.

I don't want to join the Navy,
I don't want to go to war,
I just want to hang around Piccadilly underground,
Living off the earnings of a high class lady.
I don't want a bullet in my backside,
I don't want my knockers shot away,
I just want to stay in England, jolly, jolly England,
And fornicate my fucking life away.

ROLL ME OVER

Oh, this is number one and the fun has just begun, Roll me o-ver, lay me down and do it a-gain, _____ Roll me o-ver in the clo-ver, Roll me o-ver lay me down and do it a-gain.

Oh, this is number one and the fun has just begun,
Roll me over, lay me down, and do it again.
Roll me over, in the clover,
Roll me over, lay me down, and do it again.

Oh, this is number two and his hand is on my shoe . . .

Oh, this is number three and his hand is on my knee . . .

Oh, this is number four and he's got me on the floor . . .

Oh, this is number five and he's got me dancing jive . . .

Oh, this is number six and he's got me doing tricks . . .

Oh, this is number seven and it's feeling just like heaven . . .

Oh, this is number eight and the doctor's awful late . . .

Oh, this is number nine and the twins are doing fine . . .

Oh, this is number ten and let's do it all again . . .

Oh, this is number 'leven and it's just like number seven . . .

Old Mother Hubbard went to her cupboard
To fetch her poor dog a bone.
But when she bent over, Rover drove her,
For the dog had a bone of his own.

HONEY BABE

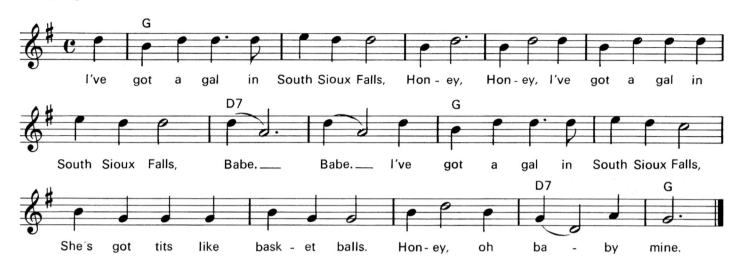

I've got a gal in South Sioux Falls, Hon-ey, Hon-ey, I've got a gal in South Sioux Falls, Babe.__ Babe.__ I've got a gal in South Sioux Falls, She's got tits like bask-et balls. Hon-ey, oh ba-by mine.

I've got a gal in South Sioux Falls,
Honey, honey,
I've got a gal in South Sioux Falls,
Babe, babe,
I've got a gal in South Sioux Falls,
She's got tits like basketballs,
Honey, oh baby mine.

I've got a gal in New Orleans . . .
All she does is lay marines . . .

I've got a gal in Tiajuana . . .
She knows how but she don't wanna . . .

I've got a gal in South Korea . . .
She's got syph and gonorrhea . . .

I've got a gal in Iowa City . . .
Not too clean and kind of shitty . . .

I've got a gal from over the hill . . .
If she won't do it her sister will . . .

I've got a gal from Boston, Mass. . . .
Makes her living with her ass . . .

I've got a gall all dressed in black . . .
She makes her money on her back . . .

I've got a gal all dressed in white . . .
She works all day and fucks all night . . .

I've got a gal in New South Bend . . .
When she's out I try her friend . . .

DO YOUR BALLS HANG LOW?

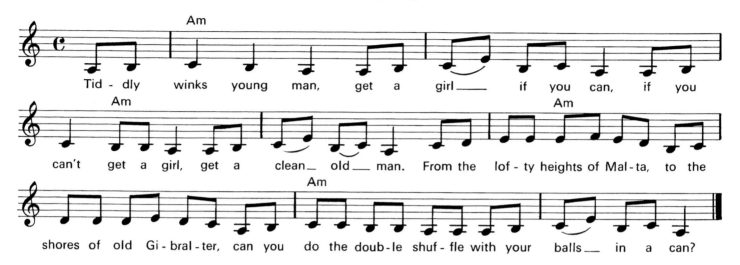

Tiddly winks, young man,
Get a girl, if you can,
If you can't find a girl
Get a clean old man.

From the lofty heights of Malta
To the shores of old Gibraltar,
Can you do the double shuffle
With your balls in a can?

Do your balls hang low,
Do they wobble to and fro,
Can you tie them in a knot,
Can you tie them in a bow?

Can you throw them over your shoulder
Like a continental soldier?
Can you do the double shuffle
If your balls hang low?

HITLER HAS ONLY GOT ONE BALL

Hitler has only got one ball.
Goering's are awfully small.
Himmler's are similar,
And Goebbels has no balls at all.

ROLL YOUR LEG OVER

I wish all young girls were bells in the tower,
And I were a Sexton, I'd bang on the hour.
  Oh, roll your leg over, roll your leg over,
  Roll your leg over the man in the moon.

I wish all them ladies was bricks in a pile,
And I were a mason, I'd lay them in style.

I wish all them ladies was little white flowers,
And I was a bee, I'd suck them for hours.

I wish all them ladies were moles in the grasses,
And I were a mole, I'd smell the molasses.

I wish all them girls were rushes a-growing,
I'd take out my scythe and start in a-mowing.

I wish all them ladies was fish in the ocean,
And I were a shark, I'd raise a commotion.

I wish all them ladies was B-29's,
And I were a fighter, I'd buzz their behinds.

I wish all them ladies was solutions to find,
And I were a frosh, I'd plug in and grind.

I wish all them ladies was dx/dt,
Then I would integrate them d-me.

I wish all them ladies was wrecks on the shoals,
Then I'd be a shipwright and plug up their holes.

I wish all them ladies were vessels of clay,
Then I'd be a potter and make them all day.

I wish all them ladies was gigantic whales,
Then I'd be a barnacle set on their tails.

I wish all young girls was bullets of lead,
Then I'd use my rifle and bang till they're dead.

I wish all young girls was telephone poles,
And I were a squirrel, I'd stuff nuts in their holes.

I wish all them ladies was statues of Venus,
And I were a Greek with a petrified penis.

I wish all them ladies was fish in a pool,
And I were a carp with a waterproof tool.

I wish all young girls were like wine in a glass
Then I'd get so drunk that I'd fall on my ass.

I wish all young girls were built like a shoe,
Then I'd be a foot and do what I could do.

I wish all them ladies was mares in a corral,
Then I'd be a stallion and make them immoral.

I wish all them ladies was bats in a steeple,
Then I'd be a bat, there'd be more bats than people.

I wish all them ladies was mares in the stable,
And I were a groom I'd mount all I was able.

I wish all them ladies was singing this song,
It'd be twice as dirty and ten times as long.

BARNACLE BILL, THE SAILOR

"Who's that knocking at my door,
Who's that knocking at my door,
Who's that knocking at my door?"
Said the fair young maiden.

"It's only me from over the sea," says Barnacle Bill the Sailor.
"My ass is tight, my temper's raw," says Barnacle Bill the Sailor.
"I'm so wound up I'm afraid to stop, I'm looking for meat or I'm going to pop,
A rag, a bone with a cherry on top," says Barnacle Bill the Sailor.

"I'll come down and let you in,"
Said the fair young maiden.

"Well, hurry before I bust the door," says Barnacle Bill the Sailor.
"I'm hard to windward and hard a-lee," says Barnacle Bill the Sailor.
"I've newly come upon the shore, and this is what I'm looking for,
A jade, a maid, or even a whore," says Barnacle Bill the Sailor.

"Oh, your whiskers scrape my cheeks,"
Said the fair young maiden.

"I'm dirty and lousy and full of fleas," says Barnacle Bill the Sailor.
"I'll stick my mast in whom I please," says Barnacle Bill the Sailor.
"My flowing whiskers give me class, the sea horses ate them instead of grass,
If they hurt your cheeks, they'll tickle your ass," says Barnacle Bill the Sailor.

"Tell me that we'll soon be wed,"
Said the fair young maiden.

"You foolish girl, it's nothing but sport," says Barnacle Bill the Sailor.
"I've got me a wife in every port," says Barnacle Bill the Sailor.
"Off I go on another tack, to give some other fair made a crack,
But keep it oiled till I come back," says Barnacle Bill the Sailor.

Way up in Pennsylvania

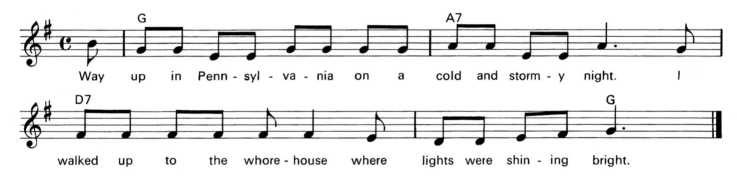

Way up in Penn-syl-va-nia on a cold and storm-y night. I
walked up to the whore-house where lights were shin-ing bright.

Way up in Pennsylvania
On a cold and stormy night,
I walked up to a whorehouse
Where lights were shining bright.

I walked across the porch
And knocked upon the door.
The knock was quickly answered
By a neatly half-dressed whore.

She wore a dark kimono
That opened down the front,
And I could see the golden hairs
That hid her filthy cunt.

She asked me what I wanted,
Her figure showed her class.
I told her all I wanted
Was a two-bit piece of ass.

She led me in the other room,
The whores were all around.
I swear it was the damndest place
That I had ever found.

I took her by her lily white hand
And led her up the stairs.
I took old Pete right in my hand
And rammed it through those hairs.

The stuff it was a-coming,
And I was feeling grand,
When I woke up in a navy-cot
With a discharge in my hand.

Cats on the Rooftops

The croc - o - dile is a fun - ny an - i - mile, He rapes his mate on - ly once in a while, But when he does he___ floods the Nile, As he rev - els in the joys of for - ni - ca - tion. Cats on the roof - tops, cats on the tiles, Cats with the clap and the crabs and the piles, Cats with their butts all wreathed in smiles, As they rev - el in the joys of for - ni - ca - tion.

The crocodile is a funny animile,
He rapes his mate only once in a while;
But when he does he floods the Nile
As he revels in the joys of fornication.

CHORUS:
Cats on the rooftops, cats on the tiles,
Cats with the clap and the crabs and the piles,
Cats with their butts all wreathed in smiles
As they revel in the joys of fornication.

Now the hippo's rump is broad and round,
One of them weighs a thousand pounds,
Two of them can quake the ground
As they revel in the throes of fornication.

The camel has a lot of fun,
His night's complete when he is done,
For he always gets two humps for one
As he revels in the throes of fornication.

The clam is a model of chastity,
You can't tell a she from a he,
But he can tell and so can she
As they revel in the throes of fornication.

The queen bees flit among the trees
And consort with whom they god damn please
And fill the world with sons of bees
As they revel in the throes of fornication.

The baboon's ass is an eerie sight,
It glows below like a neon light,
It waves like a flag in the jungle night
As he revels in the throes of fornication.

The monkey's short and rather slow,
Erect he stands a foot or so,
But when he comes it's time to go
And revel in the throes of fornication.

Five hundred verses all in rhyme,
To sing them all seems such a crime
When we could better spend our time
Revelling in the throes of fornication.

BELL BOTTOM TROUSERS

Once I was a serving maid, down in Drury Lane, My master was so kind to me, my mistress was the same, A-long came a sailor, a- shore on liberty, And oh, to my woe, he took liberty, on me singing "Bell bottom trousers, coat of navy blue. let him climb the riggin like his daddy used to do.

Once I was a serving maid, down in Drury Lane
My master was so kind to me, my mistress was the
     same;
Along came a silor ashore on liberty,
And oh, to my woe, he took liberty on me.
    Singing "Bell bottom trousers, coat of navy
       blue,
    Let him climb the rigging like his daddy used
       to do."

He asked me for a kerchief to tie around his head,
He asked me for a candle to light his way to bed;
And I, like a silly fool, not meaning any harm,
I jumped into the sailor's bed to keep the sailor warm.

He said he was no Samson but he really went to town,
He hugged me on the bed until my blue eyes turned
     to brown.
Then early in the morning, before the break of day,
A five pound note he gave me, and this to me did say:

Maybe you'll have a daughter, maybe you'll have
    a son;
Take this, oh my darling, for the damage I have done;
If you have a daughter, daff her on your knee,
And if you have a son, send the bastard off to sea."

The moral of this story is plain as plain can be:
Never let a sailor get an inch above your knee.
I trusted one once and he put off to sea
And left me with a daughter to daff upon my knee.

New words & New music adaptation by Oscar Brand.
©Copyright 1952, 1960 Oscar Brand, New York. Used by permission

MUSH, MUSH, MUSH, TOURALIADY

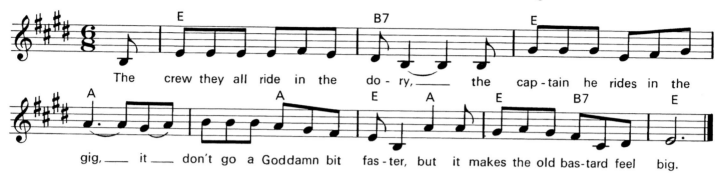

The crew they all ride in the do-ry,—— the cap-tain he rides in the gig,—— it—— don't go a Goddamn bit fas-ter, but it makes the old bas-tard feel big.

The crew they all ride in the dory,
The captain he rides in the gig,
It don't go a Goddamn bit faster
But it makes the old bastard feel big.

CHORUS:
Sing mush mush mush touraliady,
Sing mush mush mush tourali aye,
Sing mush mush mush touraliady,
Sing mush mush mush tourali aye.

The sexual life of the camel
Is greater than anyone thinks;
In moments of amorous passion
He often makes love to the Sphinx.

Now the Sphinx's posterior organs
Are blocked by the sands of the Nile
Which accounts for the hump on the camel
And the Sphinx's inscrutable smile.

In the process of civilization
From anthropoid ape down to man,
The palm is awarded the navy
For frigging whenever it can.

Exhaustive experimentation
By Darwin and Huxley and Hall
Has proved that the ass of the hedgehog
Can hardly be buggered at all.

We therefore believe our conclusion
Is incontrovertibly shown:
Comparative safety on shipboard
Is enjoyed by the hedgehog alone.

Now here's to the girls of Tri-Delta,
And here's to the streets that they roam,
And here's to their dirty-faced bastards:
God bless 'em they may be our own.

Songs That Ought Not To Be Sung

The last of the punch is getting warm and there are only a few cans of beer left in the fridge. All the Evans Hall girls have either been locked up for the night or are in their lovers pads balling. The clan has gathered back-a "Papa" Bills for a while because it's too soon to go home and too lonely a time for drifting off. So while Big Red and the rest pick up, Hock makes a fresh gimlet and strums his box softly. Quietly at first and then with increasing gusto—"A sailor told me before he died, And I never knew if the bastard lied, That he had a bride with a cunt so wide. . . ."

And so on many a night at fraternity houses, and in scattered apartments, the songs we wish we were not here to sing get belted out, until we are too tired or tanked to care. For these are truly songs that ought never be sung.

Last Night I Stayed at Home

This comparatively recent song was learned in 1956 in Pasadena from the Crud Alley Quartet. It is a sociological commentary on the result of frustration induced by the middle class mores of the 20th century American Society. It is usually sung when it would be more frustrating to even attempt to pronounce "sociological." The tune is "Funiculi, Funicula."

(16)

The Ring Dang Doo

This song is heard in two main versions today. In one, sung by Oscar Brand, the poor deceived young maiden is sent from the house to enter the oldest profession. She is so successful in this that she inflames the whole army and navy with passion and chancre. In the other version, of which this is an example, she is herself done in by one soldier who was too much for her—but her ring dang doo lives on.

The melody for this is a variant of "The Glendy Burke," but there is evidence that this song predates "The Glendy Burke" by at least half a century. *(3, 11, 17-III)*

The Winnipeg Whore

One version is from Texas, another is from California, and from all reports, the other 48 states are doing fine, too. The Chippeway River goes nowhere near the city of Winnipeg; however, this doesn't throw much doubt on the rest of the facts of the story. It is such a common one that Oscar Brand was prompted to write this additional verse as advice to all future travelers:

> In Winnipeg I learned my lesson,
> I learned it good 'cause I learned it there.
> If you gotta visit a Winnipeg whore, boys,
> Better make sure that you visit her bare. *(3, 11, 17-II)*

Columbo

One of the best known songs of the backroom drinking session is "Columbo" or "The Good Ship Venus." It has practically no plot, so the singer can choose any of the hundreds of verses he wishes. The song has a tremendous pool of verses to choose from, and more are being added all the time. One of the more inspired variants begins:

> O, the sailors looked and looked and looked
> For geishas and for sake,
> And almost gave up looking
> When they came to Nagasaki.

The verses here are collected from many sources. Some are quite new, while some may have been sung by the crew that brought the pox back from Europe. *(11)*

The Good Ship Venus (17-V)

The Big Wheel

Gershon Legman, a prominent folklorist, has this to say about the song: "Perhaps the most typical of the recent American songs is 'The Great Wheel', a gruesome story chanted solemnly to the hymn-tune 'O Master, Let Me Walk With Thee', in which the husband of the woman who 'never could be satisfied' builds a gigantic mechanical succedaneum for her, with all sorts of Detroit-style attachments, which most certainly does satisfy her . . . and this whole sorcerer's apprentice tale ends dreadfully in a fecal explosion, which can most conveniently be described in psychoanalytic terms as an anal-sadistic substitute orgasm in which the machine agencies its impotent creator by tearing the woman to bits."

118

The tune which the editors learned is different from the one Legman mentions, and it should be sung rather belligerently instead of chanted. (3, 17-VI)

The Ball of Ballynoor

A constantly requested number, this song of Scottish origin, known there as "The Ball of Kerriemuir," has since been adopted as a bit of patriotic nostalgia by all the third-generation immigrants who have their hearts in the Highlands. By the time it reached the ears of the editors it had been filtered through many rows of close-packed university students, so the reader may infer that all the verses are not in the original Scots. (11, 17-III)

Shove It Home

This is descended from a sea shanty, used for pumping ship, which had a chorus, "Put your shoulder next to mine and pump away." The tune in both cases is almost identical. This is almost certainly the ancestor of the popular WW II song, "Roll Me Over in the Clover," both textually and melodically. (2)

Kafoozalum

This is a parody of a stage song written in 1866 about Kafoozalum, a beautiful Muslim girl in love with an unbeliever. The original song is quite forgotten; however, its parody is still alive and is getting livelier as the years go on. (1, 3, 11, 17-III)

The Chisholm Trail

The chorus of this parody was learned in high school, but the informant couldn't remember any of the words (which didn't stop him from singing the song). It has always been our opinion that cowboy songs were just a little bit one hundred percent red-blooded American to be true, and perhaps the collectors have been trying to protect us from our heritage. This version has the dubious distinction that, once an editor starts wielding the blue-nose pencil, not even the chorus will remain. (1, 2, 16)

The Sixty-Nine Comes Down the Track

We have allowed ourselves the luxury of including only two songs trading upon the mysterious number. The verses of this one, being essentially rhymed couplets, are by no means exclusive to this song, and it should be easy for the singer to improvise his own—so folk songs are born. (27)

Three Whores of Winnipeg

According to folklorist Guthrie Meade, this hoary tale of the three ladies who swapped fish stories about the size of their organs is one of the few bawdy songs which can rival "The Sea Crab" in age.

O'Reilley's Daughter

This is also known as "One-Eyed Reilley" and "One-Ball Reilley." It has many different versions, some even suitable for ladies-aid tea socials—however, the singer might do well to pick his ladies-aid society carefully.

The song appeared in broadside collections at least a hundred years ago, and was probably of reasonable age even then. As is often the case, the nonsense chorus is one of the most significant parts of the song.

In T. S. Eliot's play, *The Cocktail Party*, one of the characters comes on stage and sings one verse of this song. Some scholars believe that this song may be the key to the play, just as the comic song "Finnegan's Wake" motivates Joyce's book. In the interest of promoting T. S. Eliot scholarship, we present this song for use as a supplement to the play.

(3, 11, 17-I)

Lehigh Valley

This is a typical bawdy hobo song, carried from state to state by the migrant workers. It is quite widely known even if it never gets in the record catalogues. It features a sly change of pace and some rather startling imagery; none quite so startling as the first verse, perhaps. The fifth verse is sometimes sung:

> Along came a city slicker,
> So handsome, clean and rich,
> He stole away my Nellie,
> That stinking son-of-a-bitch.

The Girls from Evans Hall

The origin of these girls changes from campus to campus, but their habits never do. As the old saw has it, "A girl from any other hall would . . ." *Sorair* gives two versions, "Girls from PCC" and "Girls from Sidney," the last being a WW II product. *(3, 17-III)*

LAST NIGHT I STAYED AT HOME

Last night I stayed at home and masturbated,
It felt so good, I knew it would.
Last night I stayed at home and masturbated,
It felt so nice, I did it twice.

You should have seen me on the short stroke,
It felt so grand, I used my hand.
You should have seen me on the long stroke,
It felt so neat, I used my feet.

Smash it, bash it,
Slam it on the floor,
Wrap it around the bedpost,
Cram it in the door.
Now there are some who say
That sexual intercourse is great,
But for maximum satisfaction
I prefer to masturbate.

THE RING DANG DOO

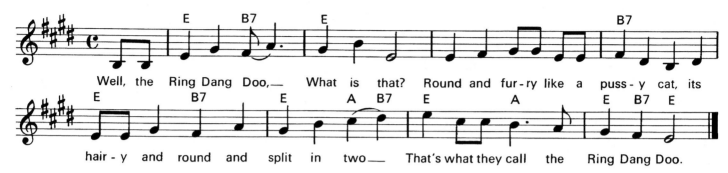

Well, the Ring Dang Doo,— What is that? Round and fur-ry like a puss-y cat, its

hair-y and round and split in two— That's what they call the Ring Dang Doo.

Well, the Ring Dang Doo, what is that?
Round and furry like a pussy cat,
It's hairy and round and split in two,
That's what they call the Ring Dang Doo.

When I was young and in my teens,
I knew a gal in New Orleans.
She was young and pretty too,
And she said she had a Ring Dang Doo.

This tender girl, a bright young maid,
Of men and boys was sore afraid.
She woke one morning with a feeling new
That there was a stranger in her Ring Dang Doo.

Her father cried from out the bed,
"Oh, dear, you've lost your maidenhead.
Go pack your bag and your satchel too,
And make your living on your Ring Dang Doo."

So she went to town to become a whore
And tacked this sign upon the door:
"A dollar down and three for two,
And you can ride on my Ring Dang Doo."

The army came and the navy went,
The price went down to fifty cents.
Still they came to get their screw
And take a ride on her Ring Dang Doo.

From out the hills came a son-of-a-bitch,
He had the clap and the seven year itch.
He had the syph and the blue balls too,
And that was the end of her Ring Dang Doo.

They tacked her tits to the courthouse wall,
They pickled her pussy in alcohol.
They buried it 'neath the avenue,
Now the busses ride on her Ring Dang Doo.

New words & music by Oscar Brand. ©Copyright 1949, 1960 Oscar Brand, New York. Used by permission.

122

THE WINNIPEG WHORE

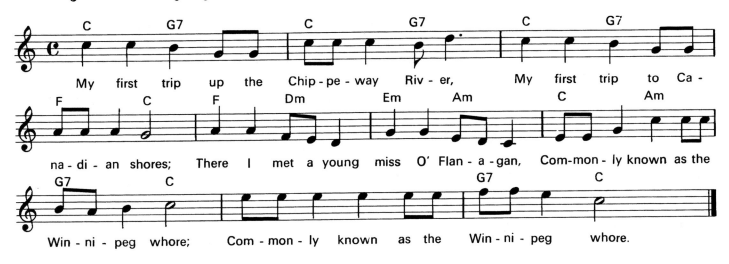

My first trip up the Chip-pe-way Riv-er, My first trip to Ca-na-di-an shores; There I met a young miss O' Flan-a-gan, Com-mon-ly known as the Win-ni-peg whore; Com-mon-ly known as the Win-ni-peg whore.

The saga of an early Canadian immigrant

My first trip up the Chippeway River,
My first trip to Canadian shores,
There I met a young Miss O'Flannigan,
Commonly known as the Winnipeg Whore. *Repeat*

"Well," says she, "I think I know you,
Let me sit upon your knee.
How's about a little lovin'?
Dollar and a half is the usual fee." *Repeat*

She took my arm and led me quickly
To the place she used for sleep.
Dirty old room with a straw-filled mattress,
Wasn't too clean but it sure was cheap.

Some were drunk and some were sober,
Some were lying on the floor.
I was in the darkest corner,
Throwing the blocks to the Winnipeg Whore.

She was fiddling, I was diddling,
Didn't know what 'twas all about.
Till I missed my watch and wallet,
Christ almighty, I found out.

Up jumped the whores and sons of bitches,
Must have been a score or more.
You'd have laughed to cream your britches
To see my ass fly out that door.

Columbo

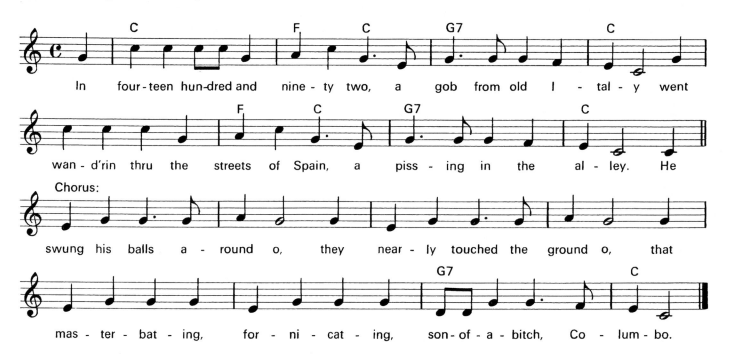

In four-teen hun-dred and nine-ty two, a gob from old I - tal - y went
wan - d'rin thru the streets of Spain, a piss - ing in the al - ley. He
Chorus:
swung his balls a - round o, they near - ly touched the ground o, that
mas - ter - bat - ing, for - ni - cat - ing, son - of - a - bitch, Co - lum - bo.

*A most ancient song concerning the voyage of the
famous Christopher Columbus. A tale told in VI parts.*

PART THE FIRST:
*In which it is explained how this voyage came about
and how the Queen of Spain tearfully bade goodbye;
Columbo's parting words to the Queen.*

In fourteen hundred ninety two
A gob from old Italy
Went wandering through the streets of Spain
A pissing in the alley.

CHORUS:
He swung his balls around-o,
They nearly touched the ground-o,
That masturbating, fornicating
Son-of-a-bitch, Columbo.

In fourteen hundred ninety two
The expedition started.
Queen Isabel, she cried like hell,
Columbo only farted.

Aboard the good ship Venus,
By God, you should have seen us,
The figurehead, a whore in bed,
The mast a throbbing penis.

PART THE SECOND:
*In which we learn more of the brave explorer,
Columbo.*

Columbo paced upon the deck,
He knew it was his duty.
He laid his whang into his hand
And said, "Ain't that a beauty."

The sailors on Columbo's ship
Had each his private knothole.
But Columbo was a superman
And used a padded porthole.

Columbo had a one-eyed cat,
He kept it in the cabin.
He rubbed its ass with axle grease
And started in a jabbing.

Columbo had a cabin boy,
That dirty little nipper!
They lined his ass with broken glass
And circumcized the skipper.

PART THE THIRD:
In which we are introduced to the crew of Venus and learn about some of their singular accomplishments.

Columbo had a first mate,
He loved him like a brother;
Every night in the pale moonlight
They buggered one another.

The second mate's name was Andy,
By God he had a dandy,
They crushed his cock between two rocks
For shooting in the brandy.

The first cook's name was Carter,
A very musical farter;
He could fart anything from God save the King
To Beethoven's Moonlight Sonata.

The bo's'ns mate fell overboard,
The sharks did leap and frolic.
Him they ate with relish great
But shortly died of colic.

PART THE FOURTH:
Concerning what the sailors did for recreation and how it came about that Columbo's daughter was lost at sea and what became of her.

The skipper's daughter Mabel
They fucked when they were able.
They tacked her tits, those homely shits,
Right to the galley table.

The skipper's other daughter
They threw into the water.
Delighted squeals revealed the eels
Had found her sexual quarter.

PART THE FIFTH:
In which the New World is at last discovered; and how the sailors expressed their joy at finding civilization.

For forty days and forty nights
They sailed the broad Atlantic.
Columbo and his lousy crew
For want of a piece were frantic.

They spied a whore upon the shore
And off came shirts and collars,
In twenty minutes by the clock
She'd made ten thousand dollars.

With joyful shout they ran about
And practiced fornication.
When they sailed they left behind
Ten times the population.

And when his men pulled out again
To take the homeward tour up,
They'd caught the pox from every box
That syphilized all Europe.

PART THE SIXTH:
In which Columbo at last returns to Spain, and how he delivers his plunder to the Queen, and the sad fate he gets for so doing.

Columbo went in haste to the Queen
Because it was his duty.
He gave to her a dose of clap;
He had no other booty.

So they threw him in a stinking jail
And left him there to grumble,
A ball and chain tied to his balls—
So ended poor Columbo.

So ends the tale.

THE GOOD SHIP VENUS

'Twas on the good-ship Ve - nus, By God you should have seen us. The fig - ure head was a whore in bed. And a mast of a phal - lic pen - is.

'Twas on the good ship Venus,
By God you should have seen us,
The figurehead was a whore in bed
And a mast of a phallic penis.

The first mate's name was Andy,
By God he had a dandy,
They crushed his cock upon a rock
For pissing in the brandy.

The second mate's name was Morgan,
By God he was a Gorgon.
From half past eight, he played till late
Upon the skipper's organ.

The cabin boy was chipper,
A likely little nipper,
He filled his ass with broken glass
And circumcized the skipper.

The captain's daughter Mabel
Would screw when she was able.
The dirty shits, they nailed her tits,
Upon the galley table.

Another daughter, Betty,
To screw was always ready,
She'd fornicate with the second mate
Upon the chartroom table.

The captain's youngest daughter
Was washed into the water.
Her plaintive squeals announced that eels
Had found her sexual quarter.

The captain's wife was Charlotte,
Born and bred a harlot,
At night her thighs were lily white,
And by morning they were scarlet.

The ship's dog's name was Rover,
We rolled that poor dog over,
And ground and ground that faithful hound
From Cape Cod back to Dover.

And when we reached our station,
In the midst of jubilation,
The ship was sunk from too much spunk
And too much fornication.

The Big Wheel

A sail-or told me be-fore he died and I nev-er knew if the bas-tard lied, that he
had a bride with a cunt so wide, the poor girl could-n't be sat-is-fied,
sat-is-fied, sat-is-fied, the poor girl could-n't be sat-is-fied.

A sailor told me before he died,
And I never knew if the bastard lied,
That he had a bride with a cunt so wide
The poor girl couldn't be satisfied.
Satisfied, satisfied,
The poor girl couldn't be satisfied.

So he fashioned a great prick out of steel
And fastened it to a fucking big wheel;
Two balls of brass were filled with cream,
And the whole fucking issue was run by steam.
Run by steam, run by steam,
The whole fucking issue was run by steam.

So round and round went the fucking big wheel,
And in and out when the great prick of steel,
Till at last she cried with a happy squeal,
"Oh, tarry awhile, I've had my fill."
Had my fill, had my fill,
Tarry awhile, I've had my fill.

But the saddest thing concerning it
Was that there was no stopping it,
Till at last she split from twat to tit,
And the whole fucking issue went up in shit.
Up in shit, up in shit,
The whole fucking issue went up in shit.

THE BALL OF BALLYNOOR

Oh, ___ the ball, ___ the ball of Bal - ly - noor, ___ Where your wife and my wife were fuck - ing on the floor, sing - ing, Who'll do ye next time. Who'll do you noo? ___ The man who did you last nicht, He can - na do you noo.

Oh, the ball,
The ball of Ballynoor,
Where your wife and my wife
Were fucking on the floor.
    Singing-a-who'll do ye next time,
    Who'll do ye noo?
    The man who did you last nicht,
    He no can do ye noo.

'Twas a gathering of the clansmen
And all the lads were there,
A-feeling up the lassies
Beneath the pubic hair.

There was doing in the parlor,
Doing on the stones,
You couldn't hear the music
For the wheezing and the groans.

There was screwing in the bedroom,
Screwing on the stair,
You couldna' see the carpet
For the mass of curly hair.

First they did it simple,
Then they tried it he's and she's;
When the ball was over
They went at it fives and threes.

They tried it on the garden path
And once around the park.
When the candles snotted out
They did it in the dark.

Mrs. John, the preacher's wife,
Was quite amazed to see
Four and twenty maidenheads
A-hangin' on the tree.

The best man in the corner
Explaining to the groom
The vagina, not the rectum,
Is the entrance to the womb.

The groom was in the corner,
Oiling up his tool,
The bride was in the icebox,
Her private parts to cool.

First lady over,
Second lady front,
Third lady's finger
Up the fourth lady's cunt.

The schoolmaster, he was there,
Going at it some,
Figurin' out by algebra
The time that he would come.

The chimney sweeper, he was there,
Of that there was no doot;
Pretty soon he farted
And he filled the air with soot.

The Deacon's wife was standing there,
Her back against the wall,
"Put your money on the tables, boys,
I'm going to fuck you all."

The Parson's wife was also there,
Sitting down in front,
A ring of posies in her hair,
A carrot up her cunt.

The letter-carrier, he was there,
The poor man had the pox,
He couldna' do the lassies
So he did the letter box.

The village idiot, he was there,
Sitting behind the band,
Amusing himself by abusing himself
And catching the drops in his hand.

The village magician cavorted around,
Doin' his vanishing trick,
He pulled his foreskin over his head
And vanished into his prick.

There were lassies wi' the syphilis
And lassies wi' the piles,
And lassies wi' their assholes
All wreathed up in smiles.

McPherson's band was there,
A-giving oot the clicks,
But you couldna' hear the music
For the swishing o' the pricks.

When the ball was over,
Everyone confessed,
The music was exquisite
But the fucking was the best.

Shove It Home

I gave her inches one,
Shove it home, shove it home,
I gave her inches one,
Shove it home;
I gave her inches one,
She said, "Johnny, ain't it fun,
Put your belly close to mine
And shove it home."

I gave her inches two,
She said, "Johnny, I love you."

I gave her inches three,
She said, "Johnny, I got to pee."

I gave her inches four,
She says, "Johnny, I want more."

I gave her inches five,
She says, "Johnny, look alive."

I gave her inches six,
She says, "I've seen bigger pricks."

I gave her inches seven,
She says, "Golly, ain't it heaven."

I gave her inches eight,
She says, "Johnny, this is great!"

I gave her inches nine,
She says, "Johnny, ain't this fine."

I gave her inches ten,
She says, "Can't you come again?"

I gave her inches twenty,
She says, "Johnny, that's a-plenty,
Put your pecker in your pants
And shove off home."

KAFOOZALUM

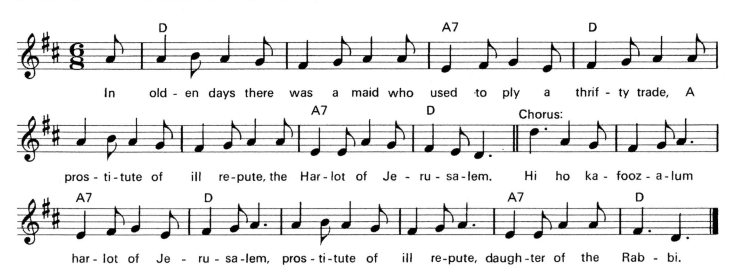

In old-en days there was a maid who used to ply a thrif-ty trade, A pros-ti-tute of ill re-pute, the Har-lot of Je-ru-sa-lem. **Chorus:** Hi ho ka-fooz-a-lum har-lot of Je-ru-sa-lem, pros-ti-tute of ill re-pute, daugh-ter of the Rab-bi.

In olden days there lived a maid who used to ply a thrifty trade,
A prostitute of ill repute, the Harlot of Jerusalem.
　　Hi, ho, Kafoozalum, the Harlot of Jerusalem,
　　Prostitute of ill repute, the daughter of the Rabbi.

She was a wily witch, a warty whore, a brazen bitch,
And every dong it got the itch, that dangled in Kafoozalum.

Nearby there lived a bastard tall with prick so hard could break a wall,
'Twas rumored he had ridden all the harlots of Jerusalem.

One day returning from a spree, a high and mighty jubilee,
Kafoozalum he chanced to see, passing thru Jerusalem.

With many a nod and glancing look she led him to a nearby brook,
And from his bulging pants she took the pride of all Jerusalem.

She took his pride with aim to please and rubbed it gently twixt her knees;
The bastard showered all the trees and drowned out half Jerusalem.

The son-of-a-bitch was underslung, he missed her hole and hit her bung,
And drove his dong into her dung, down by Jerusalem.

Now Kafoozalum, she knew her part, she cocked her ass and let a fart,
And blew that bastard like a dart, high over Jerusalem.

And there he lay, a broken mass, his cock all filled with shit and gas,
While Kafoozalum she wiped her ass, all over Jerusalem.

THE CHISHOLM TRAIL

Sad-dled old Bol-lie and head-ed for the herd. He threw me off in a fresh cow-turd.

Chorus: Gon-na tie my peck-er to a tree, to a tree, Gon-na tie my peck-er to a tree.

Saddled old Bollie and headed for the herd,
He threw me off in a fresh cow-turd.
    Gonna tie my pecker to a tree, to a tree,
    Gonna tie my pecker to a tree.

I was coming down the mountain by the old cow-trail,
With my pecker in my hand and a heifer by the tail.

The hair on her head was a piss-burnt color,
And the crabs on her ass was a-fucking one another.

I jumped from the saddle and threw her in the grass,
And pumped salvation up her dirty rotten ass.

It was damn fine doings but I ran it too close,
And I wound up with a hell of a dose.

I was in bed six weeks before they turned me loose,
Soaking my cock in tobacco juice.

Last time I saw the boss, haven't seen him since,
He was screwing a cow thru a barb-wire fence.

And now my song is ended, I can sing you no more,
There's an apple in my ass, and you can have the core.

C.T. HILL

THE SIXTY-NINE COMES DOWN THE TRACK

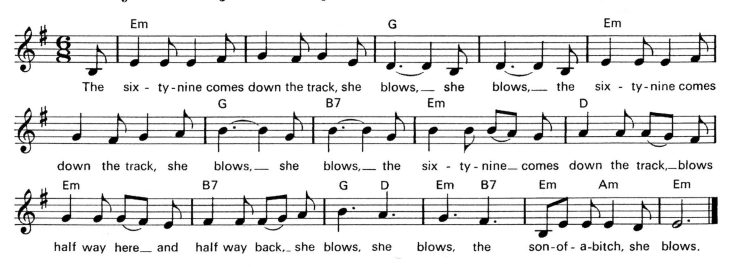

The six-ty-nine comes down the track, she blows,— she blows,— the six-ty-nine comes down the track, she blows,— she blows,— the six-ty-nine— comes down the track,—blows half way here— and half way back,— she blows, she blows, the son-of-a-bitch, she blows.

Tune: "When Johnny Comes Marching Home"

The sixty-nine comes down the track,
She blows, she blows,
The sixty-nine comes down the track,
She blows, she blows,
The sixty-nine comes down the track,
Blows halfways here and halfway back,
She blows, she blows,
The son-of-a-bitch, she blows.

The engineer is at the throttle,
Screwing himself with a whiskey bottle.

The fireman sat on the bench,
And tightened his nuts with a monkey wrench.

Lady in the dining car,
Screwing herself with a big cigar.

(Make up the next one yourself)

THREE WHORES OF WINNIPEG

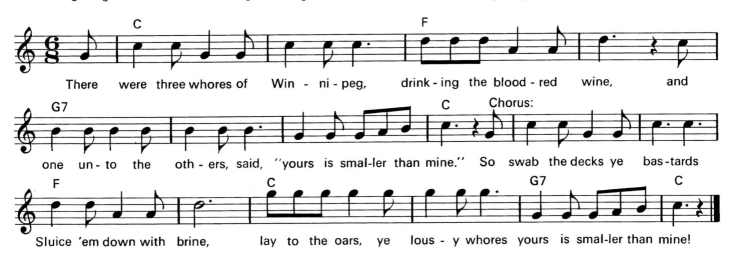

There were three whores of Win - ni - peg, drink - ing the blood - red wine, and one un - to the oth - ers, said, "yours is smal - ler than mine." So swab the decks ye bas - tards Sluice 'em down with brine, lay to the oars, ye lous - y whores yours is smal - ler than mine!

There were three whores of Winnipeg,
Drinking the blood-red wine,
And one unto the others said,
"Yours is smaller than mine."

CHORUS:
So swab the decks, ye bastards,
Sluice 'em down with brine,
Lay to the oars, ye lousy whores,
Yours is smaller than mine.

"You're a liar," said the first whore,
"Mine's as big as the air,
The fleet sails in and the fleet sails out
And never tickles a hair."

"You're a liar," said the second whore,
"Mine's as big as the sea,
The fleet sails in and the fleet sails out
And never bothers me."

"You're a liar," said the third whore,
"Mine's the biggest of all,
The fleet sails in on the first of June,
And doesn't come out till fall."

O'REILLEY'S DAUGHTER

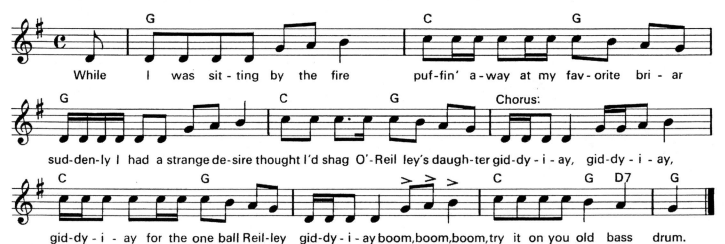

Concerning how a young man struck up an acquaintance with a fair maid, and how that suitor met her father.

When I was sitting by the fire
Puffin' away at my favorite briar,
Suddenly I had a strange desire
Thought I'd shag O'Reilley's daughter.
    Giddy-i-aye, giddy-i-aye,
    Giddy-i-aye for the one-ball Reilley,
    Giddy-i-aye, boom, boom, boom,
    Try it on your old bass drum.

Her hair was black and her eyes were blue,
The Colonel and the Major and the Captain sought her,
The Sergeant and the Private and the Drummer-boy, too,
All of them shagged O'Reilley's daughter.

While walking thru the park that day
Who should I meet but O'Reilley's daughter.
Never a word I had to say
But "Don't you think we really oughter?"

Down the stairs and into bed
I shagged and shagged until I stove her,
Never a word that maiden said,
Just laughed like hell till the fun was over.

Suddenly a footstep at the door,
Who should it be but the one-ball Reilly,
Two horse-pistols in his belt,
He was in a fit entirely.

I grabbed O'Reilley by the balls,
Shoved his head in a pail of water.
Shoved those pistols up his butt
Damn sight further than I shagged his daughter.

Now all you lasses, all you maids,
Answer now and don't speak shyly—
Would you have it straight and true,
Or the way I give it to the one-ball Reilley?

New words & music by Oscar Brand.
©Copyright 1950, 1960 Oscar Brand, New York. Used by permission.

LEHIGH VALLEY

Don't look at me that way, mis-ter, I did-n't shit in your seat, I've just come down from the moun-tain and my balls are cov-ered with sleet.

Don't look at me that way, mister,
I didn't shit in your seat.
I've just come down from the mountains
And my balls are covered with sleet.

I was up in the Lehigh Valley,
Me and my old pal Lou,
Pimping for a whorehouse
And a God-damn good one too.

It was there that I met my Nellie,
She was the village belle,
I was just a cheap panhandler,
But I loved that gal like hell.

Along came a city slicker,
So handsome, clean and rich.
He stole my pretty Nellie,
That stinking son-of-a-bitch.

But I'm just resting my ass awhile
Before I be on my way,
But I'll hunt that runt that stole my cunt
If it takes till Judgement Day.

THE GIRLS FROM EVANS HALL

We go to col-lege, to col-lege, go we; we nev-er lost our vir-gin-i-ty. We might have lost it if on-ly they forced it, we are from Ev-ans hall.

We go to college, to college go we,
We never lost our virginity.
We might have lost it if only they forced it,
We are from Evans Hall.

We go to college, to college go we,
We never lost our virginity.
We use the very best candles, you see,
We are from Evans Hall.

And every week at the Saturday dance,
We don't wear bras and we don't wear pants.
We like to give the Freshmen a chance,
We are from Evans Hall.

And every night at just twelve o'clock,
We watch the watchman piss off the dock.
We like the way he handles his cock,
We are from Evans Hall.

We go to college, we have our fun,
We know exactly the way that it's done,
We saw the movies in Hygiene A-1,
We are from Evans Hall.

We go to college, we can be had,
Don't take our word, boys, ask dear old dad,
He brings his buddies for graduate studies,
We are from Evans Hall.

Psalms For The Psacrilegious

The '60's have seen the emergence of "hate" cards and "sick" jokes; religion has received the same treatment at the hands of the singers as motherhood and apple pie. (Quick, son, drink your soup before it clots.) The University of Kansas had their own "Top Ten" list a few years ago, and number one was "Rock Around the Cross," by Pontius Pilate and the Nailers.

Perhaps the most typical of these songs is "Christianity Hits the Spot," a parody of an odious Pepsi-Cola commercial of a few years back. The choice of a song to parody is not accidental, and the parody says something about the ethics of advertising as well as organized religion. This is the spirit in which most of these songs are sung. The singer is most likely to be a sophomore in college who is just learning that all things aren't either black or white, and who is having real doubts about his beliefs. They are not so likely to be sung by the Jr. High crowd (still naive Christians) or by the grad students (cynical atheists). But, like most of the songs in this book, they are meant to be sung, not talked about, so—lift up your chalice and join in!

The Ballad of Jesus Christ

This was printed in *The Bosses Songbook: Songs to Quench the Flames of Discontent*, published in New York as a wry rejoinder to the IWW songbook, *Songs of the Workers*, subtitled "Songs to Fan the Flames of Discontent." Woody Guthrie wrote a real (non-blasphemous) "Ballad of J.C." to the same tune, "Jesse James," and this is probably a parody of that song. (*15, 16*)

I Am Jesus' Little Lamb

Rumor credits the composition of this to a student at Loyola, the Jesuit University in Chicago. If this is true, it only points out the speed with which such songs spread, for it has been collected at colleges on both coasts as well as the Midwest in the last five years. The tune is "Twinkle, Twinkle, Little Star."

Christianity Hits the Spot

This little ditty is sung to the tune of the now defunct Cola commercial. It can be applied to other religions as desired.

138

THE BALLAD OF JESUS CHRIST

'Bout____ three or four B. C., By the sea of Gal - i - lee washed in his un - wed mo - ther's tears, he____ fought the rul - ing clas-ses, preached the gos - pel to the mas - ses, and pre - dat - ed Marx by eight - een hund - red years.

Chorus:
Poor Je - sus had no wife, to mourn for his life, he need - ed a bath and a shave but that ene - my of the prole-tari - at, Ju - das is - car - iat, he laid poor Je - sus in his grave.

Tune: "Jesse James"

'Bout three or four B.C.
By the sea of Galilee,
Washed in his unwed mother's tears,
He fought the ruling classes,
Preached the Gospel to the masses,
And pre-dated Marx by eighteen hundred years.
    Poor Jesus had no wife
    To mourn for his life,
    He needed a bath and a shave;
    But that enemy of the proletariat,
    Judas Iscariat,
    He laid poor Jesus in his grave.

I AM JESUS' LITTLE LAMB

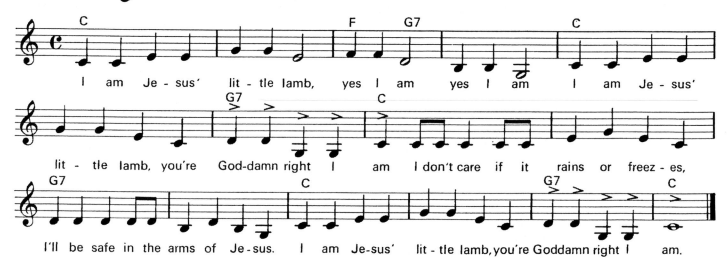

I am Jesus' little lamb, yes I am, yes I am,
I am Jesus' little lamb,
You're God damn right I am!

I don't care if it rains or freezes,
I'll be safe in the arms of Jesus.
I am Jesus' little lamb,
You're God damn right I am!

CHRISTIANITY HITS THE SPOT

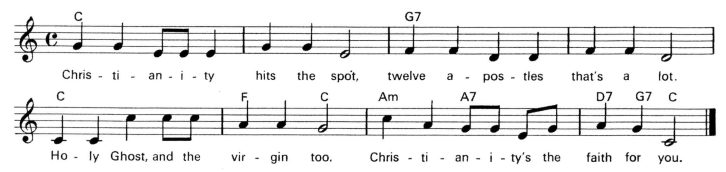

Christianity hits the spot,
Twelve apostles, that's a lot.
Holy Ghost and the Virgin too—
Christianity's the faith for you!
(Holy, holy, holy, holy)

Judaism hits the spot,
Ten commandments, that's a lot.
Patriarch Moses and a Talmud too—
Judaism is the faith for you!
(Torah, Torah, Torah, Torah)

BIBLIOGRAPHY AND DISCOGRAPHY

The following bibliography and discography should not be considered a complete list of all the published versions of these songs. It is rather an acknowledgement of our particular sources, together with the abbreviation given in the text for the most frequently used references.

Most of the songs in this book are collated from several sources, written, oral and recorded. Since there are very strict limits on how far one can go in print or on record, it goes without saying that much of the material in this volume must be, by its very nature, transmitted only orally.

With each song we have prepared notes which include the written and recorded sources; we have included only the sources which might be available in libraries or in private collections. The oral sources have been left out purposely—they are none of the reader's business. If he wants an oral source, he should find himself a party, sing part of the first verse, and say, "Does anyone know the rest of this song?" If it doesn't work, he is merely at the wrong party—try next door.

BIBLIOGRAPHY

1: *Typical Specimens of Vulgar Folklore.* From the collection of Gershon Legman. Typed MS by Kenneth Larson, Salt Lake City, 1952. From the Folklore Archives, Indiana University.

2: *Barnyard Folklore of Southeastern Idaho.* Typed MS by Kenneth Larson, Salt Lake City, 1952. From the Indiana University Folklore Archives.

3: *Songs of Raunch and III Repute.* Mimeographed songbook, compiled at Cal Tech, Pasadena, 1958.

4: *Shanties from the Seven Seas.* Stan Hugill. Dutton, 1958.

5: *Songs of American Sailormen.* Joanna C. Colcord. Bramhall House, New York, 1958.

6: *Irish Street Ballads.* Colm O'Lochlainn. Citadel Press, 1960

7: *Wit & Mirth; or Pills to Purge Melancholy.* Edited originally by Henry Playford, with subsequent additions by Thomas D'Urfey.

8: *Ed McCurdy's Song Book of Wit and Mirth.* Ed McCurdy. Hargail Music Press, New York, 1963.

9: *Merry Muses of Caledonia.* Robert Burns, Burns Federation, 1911. From text published ca. 1800.

10: *The Merry Muses of Caledonia.* Robert Burns. Edited by James Barke and Sydney Goodsir Smith. G. P. Putnam's Sons, New York, 1959.

11: *Bawdy Songs and Backroom Ballads.* Oscar Brand. Dorchester Press, 1960.

12: *The Sea Crab.* Guthrie T. Meade. Midwest Folklore, 1959, Vol. VII, No. 2.

13: *Reliques of Ancient English Poetry, Vol. II.* Thomas Percy, 1812.

14: *Personal Choice.* Ewan MacColl. Hargail Music Press.

15: *The Boss' Songbook*

16: *Song Fest.* Edited by Dick and Beth Best. Crown Publishers, Inc., New York, 1955.

DISCOGRAPHY

17: *Bawdy Songs and Backroom Ballads,* Vol. I, II, III, IV, V, VI. Oscar Brand. Audio Fidelity.

18: *When Dalliance Was In Flower,* Vol. I, II, III, IV. Ed McCurdy. Elektra Records.

19: *Son of Dalliance.* Ed McCurdy. Elektra Records.

20: *Merry Muses of Caledonia.* Paul Clayton. Elektra Records.

21: *Unholy Matrimony.* Paul Clayton. Elektra Records.

22: *Scots Drinking Songs.* Ewan MacColl. Riverside.

23: *English Street Songs.* A. L. Lloyd. Riverside.

24: *Pills to Purge the Melancholy.* Will Holt. Stinson.

25: *The Seeds of Love.* Andrew Roland Summers. Folkways.

26: *The Fireside Book of Favorite American Songs.* Margret Boni. Simon & Schuster, New York, 1952.

FOR YOUR FURTHER ENJOYMENT

Blow, Boys, Blow. Ewan MacColl and A. L. Lloyd.

Leadbelly Memorial. Huddie Ledbetter. Stinson.

Sonny Terry. Sonny Terry. Riverside.

Irish Drinking Songs. Patrick Galvin. Riverside.

Every Inch a Sailor. Oscar Brand. Elektra Records.

Songs My Mother Never Taught Me. J. J. Niles, D. S. Moore, A. A. Wallgren. Macaulay, 1929.

Shantymen and Shantyboys. William Main Doerflinger. Macmillan Company, New York, 1951.

INDEX